Israel's Ten Lost Tribes
in Japan
and throughout Asia

International Symposium 2025

September 14-16

Tachikawa, Tokyo

By the Bible and Japan Forum & Lost Tribes Institute

2025

Israel's Ten Lost Tribes
in Japan
and throughout Asia
International Symposium 2025

By the Bible and Japan Forum together with Lost Tribes Institute

Published by Lost Tribes Institute.
Los Angeles, CA, USA
First Edition, 2025.
ISBN: 978-1-959466-16-1
eBook ISBN 978-1-959466-17-8

Table of Contents

Symposium Introduction by Arimasa Kubo

(September 14, 2025)

Hello, everyone,
I am truly delighted to have the opportunity to welcome people from the descendants of the lost tribes of Israel, such as those from Kyrgyzstan, India, Mizoram, and the ethnic Karen, as well as the founder of the Lost Tribes Research Institute. I believe this is an event of such historical significance that it could be considered one of the greatest moments in history.

As Anchalee from the Karen people in Thailand mentioned, the Karen, like us Japanese, have their own calendar, the Karen calendar, in addition to the commonly used one. The Karen's concept of time begins in 739 BCE, which marks the year of the first Assyrian captivity when the Assyrian Empire invaded the Northern Kingdom of Israel and took away the three tribes of Gad, Reuben, and Manasseh from the east side of the Jordan River. In other words, the Karen people designate that year as the start of their wandering era.
The Karen also have a memory of a lost sacred scripture. This lost sacred scripture refers to the Torah scroll. In ancient times, before the invention of printing, a tribe would be fortunate to possess even one Torah scroll. This memory of a lost sacred scripture is not unique to the Karen people; it is also found among the Mizo and Chin tribes in India, the Yi minority in China, and the Kyrgyz in Central Asia. It is a common theme among the descendants of the lost tribes.

Does Japan have such a memory of a lost sacred scripture? Yes, it does. Historical records state that in 645 CE, a Buddhist faction set fire to the imperial library, burning most of the important texts stored there. In other words, more than 60 years before the appearance of the oldest known Japanese texts, like the *Kojiki* or *Nihon Shoki*, the imperial warehouse contained many valuable texts. Jewish studies scholar Joseph Eidelberg suggests that among those texts could have been a Torah scroll. After this incident, the Shinto faction gained power, and a major reform, similar to the Meiji Restoration, called the Taika Reform, was carried out. During this time, the emperor issued various teachings, many of which seem to reference the Torah. For more details, this is written in Joseph Eidelberg's book *The Biblical Hebrew Origin of the Japanese People*.

Since ancient times, Japan has had the term "Torah no Maki" (the Scroll of the Torah). This refers to the Torah scroll, which is traditionally considered the most important truth given by the mountain god Tengu to ninjas. This legend actually originated in Central Asia. The people of the famous Hata tribe, who originally lived in Central Asia, brought stories of Tengir and the Torah scroll to Japan. Richard Hewitt, who lived in Kyrgyzstan for a long time, knows this well. In that mountainous region, God is referred to as Tengu or Tengir. The

God of the Bible, who gave the law to Moses on Mount Sinai, is also a mountain god, so the Torah scroll originally refers to the Torah, the sacred scripture.

As Anchalee also mentioned, the Karen people have called the God of Creation "Yuwa" (Y'wa). Not only the Karen but also the descendants of the lost tribes have referred to God as "Yua" or "Ya." This comes from the name of God, "Yahweh." This is the same in Japan. Among Japanese Shinto priests, the pronunciation "Ya" has always been considered sacred. "Ya" is a shortened form of "Yah," as in "Hallelujah," which means "Praise Ya" or "Glorify Ya" in the Bible.

The names of Japanese shrines also reflect this, such as Ya-saka Shrine, Ya-hata Shrine, or Ya-tsurugii Shrine. These names are sacred because of the sound "Ya."

In Shimane Prefecture, there is the Izumo Taisha, a massive shrine known for the "Yakumo" (Eight Clouds) mentioned in songs as standing above the shrine. The Bible describes a pillar of cloud standing above Moses' Tabernacle. Similarly, it is said that a pillar of cloud stood above Izumo Taisha. However, this does not mean "eight clouds." The ceiling of Izumo Taisha's main hall is painted with an image of Yakumo, but publicly available photos show only seven clouds. Therefore, Yakumo does not mean "eight clouds" but rather "Ya's cloud."

As I mentioned before, in Takasago City, Hyogo Prefecture, there is a shrine called Sone Tenmangu where an annual festival called "Hitotsumono" is held grandly. "Hitotsumono" means "the one and only thing." During this festival, a boy appears surrounded by young men dressed in Middle Eastern-style clothing. The boy is accompanied by his parents, a scene reminiscent of Joseph and Mary. The young men in Middle Eastern-style clothing

repeatedly shout, "Yoi, yoi, be!" When asked what this means, the response is, "We don't know, it's just tradition." However, to us, it sounds like the Hebrew phrase "Yom Yobel," meaning "the day of Jubilee." Therefore, Dr. Tetsu called this festival the "Feast of Christ."

During this festival, the boy appears with a large "Ya" character written on his forehead. The reading of "Ya" as "eight" comes from Chinese origins, but in ancient Japanese (Yamato) language, it should be read as "Ya." The Bible says, "Blessed is the one who comes in the name of Ya," referring to the Messiah. Thus, the "Ya" character on the boy's forehead signifies that he is the Messiah who came in the name of Ya.

There are many other connections between Japan, the lost tribes of ancient Israel, and ancient Eastern Christianity. Japan's roots lie there. I hope you will learn more about this through this symposium. Thank you.

Arimasa Kubo (September 14, 2025)

Welcome

By Hideo Hatakeda

to the 2025 Ten Lost Tribes Tokyo Conference

Greetings from the Chairman of “the Bible and Japan Forum”

In Tokyo, the capital of Japan, the land of the rising sun, we are able to welcome together with us "descendants of the ten lost tribes" who believe in God the Creator and His only Son, Jesus Christ.

Our meeting may seem like a tiny pea to the world, like the apostle John and Peter throwing a single stone across the Sea of Galilee. However, if we can see through the eyes of God, who is in charge of history, how can we see it today in the year 2025, 2,000 years after Jesus came to this world? For those who believe in the Old and New Testaments as the Word of God, the nation of Israel is a nation that emerged as God's chosen nation. However, that nation was destroyed. It was lost and scattered throughout the world. But, but. The Bible prophesies:

Paul said in Romans 11, "All Israel shall be saved."

Also、John wrote in Revelation 7:1-2
And after these things I saw four angels standing on the four corners of the earth, holding the four winds of the earth, that the wind should not blow on the earth, nor on the sea, nor on any tree.
And I saw another angel ascending from the east, having the seal of the living God;and he cried with a loud voice to the four angels, to whom it was given to hurt the earth and the sea
Saying, Hurt not the earth, neither the sea, nor the trees, till we have sealed the servants of our God in their foreheads.
And John saw, "I heard the number of those who were sealed, 144,000, of every tribe of the children of Israel."
First, the tribe of Judah, 12,000.
The tribe of Reuben, 12,000.
Finally, Joseph, 12,000, and Benjamin, 12,000.

These numbers are symbolic, the perfect number that God is seeking.

There is a beginning to everything. When the Savior, Jesus, was born, an angel called to Mary, "Behold, you will conceive in your womb and give birth to a son, and you shall call his name Jesus." Luke 1:31

And when the time came, Jesus was born into this world.

The origins of the Bible and Japan Forum

Our Bible and Japan Forum was conceived here in Japan in 1992, just 33 years ago, when around 30 people on the shores of Lake Hamana searched for the roots of the Japanese people and raised the idea that those roots might lie in Israel, the land of the Bible. Protestant pastor Yutaka Koishi was the first president. The following year, in 1993, conferences and training seminars were officially launched. All of these events are recorded, totaling 222. Over the 33 years since its inception, this forum has progressed while tracing the traces of Israel throughout Japan.

Even amid the COVID-19 pandemic that engulfed the entire world, our meetings had not been suspended. I am extremely pleased that on this day in September 2025, we have been able to welcome all of you descendants of the Ten Lost Tribes who were scattered around the world on your way from Israel to Japan, and that we have been able to hold our first-ever conference, face-to-face gathering, and symposium.

This meeting is different from any other meeting in the world. This meeting is not an ordinary meeting. When Jesus was 12 years old, he went up to Jerusalem with his parents, but he got separated from them. His parents searched for him for three days. Now Jesus was in the temple, sitting in the midst of the teachers, listening to them and asking them questions.

In Luke 2:49 he asked his parents, “How is it that you sought me? Did you not know that I must be about my Father's business?”

We are gathered here as we should be. From here we will take the final step towards the salvation of Israel and the whole world in order to fulfill God's prophecy. We pray that God's Will will be carried forward through this conference, and our hope is the salvation of each individual soul.

Our goal is not simply the study and research of history. Of course, knowing that God's hand is at work in history is meaningful because it confirms what God is actually doing.

However, what we as human beings desire more is for each and every person to live their life with new hope. This is not only the salvation of our souls from sin, but also the salvation of the nation to which each person belongs.

It is the salvation of each country, America, Russia, China, Britain, Europe, Asia, and Africa. As it is written in the Book of Revelation in the Bible, I want to see with my own eyes the image of the heavenly city. The appearance of the kingdom of heaven is described as follows:

"The nations will walk in the glory of God, and the kings of the earth will bring their glory into it. Its gates will never be closed all day, for there will be no night there. And they will bring into it the glory and honor of the nations" (Revelation 21:24-26).

It has been promised that the nations of the world will come to the Kingdom of Heaven with their own glory and honor -- in other words, with their historical heritage, culture, traditions, and the honor of their cultural assets worthy of the Kingdom of Heaven. For this reason, we do not simply study a country's culture; we dig deep into the traces of the Bible in each country in order to preach the gospel of Jesus, while honouring the treasures found throughout the country, in the hope that each person's soul will be completely transformed and they will be able to walk through life with a renewed heart. It is my heartfelt prayer that God's powerful hand will touch not only those gathered here, but also each and every one of you who are participating remotely.

This concludes my opening remarks. Thank you very much,

Hideo Hatakeda

Israel-Mizo Identity

By Dr. P.C. Biaksiama

A Review of Zaithanchhungi's Book for the 1st Scientific Symposium

Introduction

The Lushai, part of the Tibeto-Burman group, share a common origin with other clans but have developed distinct cultural and linguistic patterns, suggesting long periods of independence. Their society, despite existing in relative isolation, exhibits traits of nobility, bravery, and hospitality, which are hallmarks of advanced human relationships. Remarkably, the Lushai's enthusiastic adoption of Christianity raises curiosity about their resistance to earlier influences like Buddhism or Confucianism, despite likely intermittent contact with their adherents throughout history.[^1]

A system of community obligation, known as "Tlawmngaihna," emphasized public service. This included tending crops for the sick, weeding the Chief's land, and rebuilding homes lost to fire. A good citizen was defined by their readiness to meet essential community needs.[^2]

The Lushai customs reflect a sophisticated code of family and social relations, accompanied by extensive ceremonies and sacrifices, indicating a highly organized societal structure.[^3]

Ceremonies and Supernatural Beliefs

Lushai ceremonies mark significant life events, including birth, death, illness, hunting, crop calamities, unnatural deaths, childbirth, and war. This constant association with the supernatural underscores their orderly, religious, and revered societal character.[^4]

Chhinlung: The Mizo Origin

All Mizos claim "Chhinlung" as their original homeland, potentially linked to "Sinlung," a township in Szechuan Province, Central China (located at 10°3' North, 31° East).[^5] Folk songs suggest their ancestors fled Sinlung due to enemies and express longing for their homeland:

"Strange are the faces and no friends they are,

I had to leave Sinlung my home."[^6]

"The famous Sinlung is my home,

The land of my father and mother;

To call it back if were possible,

The land of my father and mother."[^7]

Around 820 AD, a Chinese prince named "Chinlung" may have ruled over the Mizos among other subjects. During this period, Buddhism spread across Burma, Siam, Malaysia, Thailand, China, and Japan, prompting some groups, possibly including Israelite descendants, to relocate to safer areas like Chengdu, west of Chongqing. Towns such as "Lushien" and "Loshan" may be the origin of the Lushai (Lusei) Mizos, who were cave dwellers at the time.[^8]

Parchment

Recent discoveries of Jewish villages or colonies possessing the "Pentateuch" in Chengdu, near "Lushien" and "Loshan," suggest these settlers may have been known as "Lusei" or "Lushai." This supports the possibility of a shared history with the Mizos.[^9] Oral tradition holds that God gave the Mizos a written language on parchment, which was lost when a dog ate it, leaving them without a written script.[^10][^11]

Religion

The Lushai believed in a supreme spirit, "Parthian," the Giver and Preserver of Life, described as "zaidam" (good-natured, amiable, humble) but relatively inactive in controlling evil spirits.[^12] Before Christianity, the Mizos worshipped "Parthian" as the Creator of the world.[^13]

Paradise

Similar to Jewish beliefs, the Mizos believe in a "Deadman's Village (Seol)" and a paradisiacal place called "Pialral."[^14]

Devil/Satan

The Mizos believe in malevolent supernatural beings called "Ramhual," akin to the Jewish concept of Satan as a symbol of evil forces.[^15]

Sacrifice

The Lushai used unblemished mithuns (bison), goats, and fowls for sacrifices, mirroring Jewish practices. Their bamboo altar, basket-shaped with four upward-projecting strips resembling the horns of a Jewish altar, was placed outside the village on a hillock. Special washing with clean water preceded sacrifices, which were primarily for healing the sick and performed by men from the patient's family. The priest smeared blood on the patient's forehead and arms. Family sacrifices to "Parthian" included prayers such as:

1. "Parthian from above, we, the sons of Manasia, offer you the blood of an animal."
2. "God of our forefathers, God of our grandmothers, respond to our sacrifice."[^16]

Priests, typically from the "Haulmar" clan among the Lusei and Sailo, were divided into:

1. "Bawlpu": Offered sacrifices for the sick across all clans, receiving meat as payment.
2. "Sadawt" (or "Sadot"): Handled religious sacrifices specific to each clan.[^17]

In 1929, during the "Chapchar Kut" festival, Brig. Ngurliana Sailo described accompanying a priest to Buallawn village's outskirts for a sacrifice. Upon returning, they identified themselves as "children of Manasia" to gain entry to the Chief's house.[^18]

Manase/Manasia

The name "Manasia" or "Manase" frequently appears in Mizo sacrificial chants and oral traditions, indicating a connection to the biblical tribe of Manasseh:

1. At family offerings: "The children of Manase offer Thee animal's blood, O, God of High."
2. For a sick person: "If tied, untie him, if manacled, unlock him, we are taking Manase home."
3. For epilepsy: "Release him, we are above your power, we are children of Manase."
4. For a tabooed paddy field: "Go away, go away, we are bringing Manase here."

5. When clearing land: "You are obstructing our grandfather Manasia."

6. Oral history mandates: "Whenever you pray to God, the name of our forefather Manesia must be pronounced."

7. For sin offerings: "God of heaven and of the earth, we, sons of Manasia, who are on earth are offering the heart, the liver of the animal for forgiveness of our sins."[^19]

Marriages and Divorce

Mizo wedding and marriage traditions share parallels with ancient Israelite practices. On the wedding day, the bridegroom sends two representatives to finalize and pay the bride price to her parents.[^20] "Levirate marriage" was practiced, where a widow married her deceased husband's unmarried brother, similar to Jewish customs (Genesis 38).[^21]

In divorce, a Mizo man could simply declare, "I divorce you," and the woman was divorced, akin to Israelite practices (Deuteronomy 24:1–2).[^22]

Death and Burial

Mizo and Jewish traditions share striking similarities in death and burial practices, suggesting a possible shared ancestry or historical coexistence.[^23] Zaithanchhungi concludes: "It is really surprising that Jews and Mizos should have detailed similarities in customs and practices regarding death and burial. And it naturally leads one to consider the probability of their being of same descendants or the possibilities that they might have lived together in the long past."[^24]

Other Conclusions

Before Christianity, the Mizos believed in a single Almighty God, Creator of everything, residing in heaven, a belief shared with the Israelites. This may explain their resistance to other religions like Buddhism.[^25] Despite living among diverse cultures over millennia, Mizo traditions align more closely with Israelite practices than with Mongolian, Chinese, or Burmese cultures. Zaithanchhungi suggests that the Mizos and Israelites likely coexisted in China, with intermarriages diluting their purity but preserving shared cultural elements.[^26]

Source Information

The content is predominantly from Zaithanchhungi's book, with minor changes and illustrations added.

- English Edition: Israel-Mizo Identity: Mizos (Chhinlung Tribes) Children of Menashe are the Descendants of Israel (out of print, limited copies available).

- Mizo Edition: Available for 250 INR at Hope Lodge, Electric Veng, Aizawl, Mizoram, India.

Footnotes

[^1]: Page 9, quoting Lushai Chrystal's, pp. 97–98, by Major A.G. McCall.

[^2]: Page 11–12, quoting Lushai Chrystal's, pp. 97–98, by Major A.G. McCall.

[^3]: Page 12, quoting Lushai Chrystal's, p. 118, by Major A.G. McCall.

[^4]: Page 12, quoting Lushai Chrystal's, p. 118, by Major A.G. McCall.

[^5]: Page 15.

[^6]: Page 15.

[^7]: Page 15.

[^8]: Page 16.

[^9]: Page 20, quoting The Origin of Mizos, Chap. 2, by Lt. Col. C.G. Vengheese, V.S.M.

[^10]: Page 20, quoting Wind Through the Bamboo: The Story of Transformed Mizos, p. 5, by Donna Strom.

[^11]: Page 21, quoting The Life and Witness of the Church in Mizoram, p. 23, by Rev. Dr. C.L. Hminga.

[^12]: Page 23, quoting The Diary of a Jungle Missionary, p. 37, by Rev. Enoch Lewis Mendus, 1888–1982.

[^13]: Page 25, quoting Wind Through the Bamboo: The Story of Transformed Mizos, p. 21, by Donna Strom.

[^14]: Page 28.

[^15]: Page 28.

[^16]: Page 35.

[^17]: Page 36.

[^18]: Page 36, signed by Brig. Ngurliana Sailo, son of the Chief of Ratu and Buallawn, DOB 1/1/1910.

[^19]: Pages 42–43.

[^20]: Page 49–50, quoting A Monograph on Lushai Customs and Ceremonies, p. 23, by N.E. Perry, I.C.S.

[^21]: Page 53, quoting Chin-Lushai Land, p. 149, 1st Edition: 1893, by Sgt. Lt. Col. A.S. Reid, M.B.

[^22]: Page 53, quoting A Monograph on Lushai Customs and Ceremonies, Chap. III, by N.E. Perry, I.C.S.

[^23]: Page 56.

[^24]: Page 63.

[^25]: Page 27.

[^26]: Page 17.

The Biblical Breeze Blowing Through the East

Dr. Kengo Nagami

Unraveling the Mystery of the Lost Ten Tribes and the Origins of the Japanese People

Introduction

Hi everyone! Today, I'd like to share some thoughts on a topic I've been exploring for many years: the connection between the Japanese and the Jewish people. In particular, I'll be talking about how ancient religious ideas may have crossed paths, and how traces of Israelite traditions might still be found in Japanese customs and cultural roots.

It's truly fascinating to consider how, over the course of history, Asia and the West have interacted—not just through trade and travel, but in ways that shaped religion, culture, and even bloodlines. In this talk, I'll walk you through a few key points: how Buddhism evolved, how Western religions entered China during the Tang Dynasty, how the Lost Ten Tribes of Israel may have spread along the Silk Road, and finally, how certain aspects of Japanese genetics and Shinto rituals show surprising similarities to ancient Israelite practices.

1. The Transformation of Buddhism and the Influence of Foreign Religions

As many of you probably know, about 600 years after the passing of the Buddha—around the late 1st to 2nd century CE—Buddhism went through a major transformation. Up until then, Theravāda Buddhism had focused mainly on personal enlightenment through rigorous self-discipline. It was, in a sense, atheistic—centered more on practice than on divine beings.

But during this period, Mahāyāna Buddhism emerged. The name itself means "Great Vehicle," symbolizing a broader path that could carry many people toward salvation. Mahāyāna followers began referring to the older tradition as "Hīnayāna," or "Lesser Vehicle," criticizing it for offering limited salvation. Behind this shift was a growing tendency to incorporate divine or god-like elements into Buddhist teachings.

Interestingly, Mahāyāna Buddhism began embracing the idea of an eternal Buddha—a divine figure—which marked a move toward theism, and even hints of monotheism. For example, the belief in Amitābha Buddha and the future Buddha Maitreya shows clear influences from West Asian religious thought and early Christianity.

Maitreya, whose name traces back to "Maitreya" in Sanskrit, is thought to be connected to the Iranian god Mithra. Some scholars also see echoes of the Christian idea of the Second Coming, as taught by the Apostle Thomas. Maitreya came to be seen as a messianic figure who would bring salvation to the people.

On the other hand, the faith in Amitābha Buddha was shaped by Thomas's teachings in India, particularly the idea that "those who call upon the name of the Lord shall be saved." This led to the concept of salvation through chanting the Buddha's name—a belief in "other-power" rather than self-effort.

Amitābha actually has two original names: Amitābha and Amitāyus. Both appear in the same scriptures and refer to the same Buddha. The first means "Infinite Light," and the second means "Infinite Life." Even in texts like the Amitābha Sutra, both aspects are explained, but in Chinese translations, the name is simply rendered phonetically as "Amituo," without delving into the deeper meanings.

"That which was from the beginning, which we have heard, which we have seen with our eyes, which we have looked at and touched with our hands—concerning the Word of life. Life appeared; we have seen it and testify to it, and we proclaim to you eternal life, which was with the Father and has appeared to us. We proclaim to you what we have seen and heard, so that you also may have fellowship with us. And our fellowship is with the Father and with his Son, Jesus Christ. We write this to make our joy complete."

Krishna and Christ

The influence of early Eastern Christianity on the Hindu god Krishna is a fascinating topic. Like the Buddha Vairocana, Krishna is a prominent deity in India. In Hinduism, one of the principal gods is Vishnu, often associated with the sun. Krishna is considered an incarnation of Vishnu—much like how, in Christianity, Christ is seen as the incarnation of God the Father, Yahweh.

Krishna appears in the Indian epic Bhagavad Gita, which is believed to have been written around the 1st or 2nd century CE. Interestingly, this timeframe overlaps with the period when Christianity was rapidly spreading in India, thanks to apostles like Thomas and Bartholomew.

What's even more intriguing is that many passages in the Bhagavad Gita describing Krishna seem to echo verses from the Gospel of John in the New Testament. Scholar John Stewart has created detailed comparison charts showing these parallels.

He suggests that Krishna worship may have emerged as a response by Brahmin priests who were unsettled by the growing influence of Christianity in India. In their search for a divine figure who could rival Jesus Christ, they shaped Krishna into a sacred counterpart. In this view, Krishna is essentially a Brahmin version of Christ—Krishna, or Christos in Greek.

Nestorian Christians in Japan

As mentioned earlier, Nestorian Christians—followers of the Church of the East—had already arrived in China by the 6th century. But they didn't stop there. By the same period, they had also reached the

Korean Peninsula. In fact, in southwestern Korea, archaeologists discovered an ancient cave with about 16 decorative panels on its inner walls, featuring Nestorian-style artwork. This cave was built in the 7th century to honor a Nestorian monk known as the "Black Monk," who had come to Korea in the 500s.

Nestorian Christians had also made their way to Japan by around the year 600. Professor Sakae Ikeda of Kyoto University, a leading scholar on Nestorianism, wrote that one of Prince Shōtoku's close advisors was a Nestorian named Mar Thoma. This was published in a newsletter from the Assyrian Church of the East. Professor Ikeda even tried to revive Nestorian churches in Japan and maintained contact with the Church's headquarters in Iraq, which confirmed this connection in their official publications.

According to the Shoku Nihongi (a historical chronicle from the 8th century), a Persian man named Rimitsuei—said to be both a physician and a Nestorian—arrived in Japan in June of 736. He was accompanied by another figure named Kōho, who is believed to have been a high-ranking member of the Nestorian Church.

Why do scholars think they were Nestorians? Because after their arrival, Emperor Shōmu and Empress Kōmyō began initiating projects that were distinctly Nestorian in nature. Emperor Shōmu used the term "Keifuku"—a Nestorian phrase meaning "universal blessing"—and began building kokubunji temples across Japan, modeled after Nestorian monasteries in China.

Empress Kōmyō, meanwhile, founded temples focused on the concept of "atonement," which is not originally part of Buddhist doctrine. She also introduced kaekae—a ritual of repentance inspired by Nestorian teachings. Her charitable work resembled that of figures like Florence Nightingale or Mother Teresa, as she devoted herself to welfare and humanitarian efforts.

All of this suggests that many practices we've long assumed to be purely Buddhist may actually have roots in other traditions. Even the Bible speaks to this kind of spiritual blending. In Acts 17:22–23, the Apostle Paul addresses the people of Athens:

"People of Athens, I see that in every way you are very religious. As I walked around and looked carefully at your objects of worship, I even found an altar with this inscription: 'To an unknown god.' So you are ignorant of the very thing you worship—and this is what I am going to proclaim to you."
That altar, according to tradition, was built during a time of disaster. The people had prayed to all the known gods, but nothing changed. So they built an altar to an "unknown god"—and the disaster ceased. Paul saw this as a perfect teaching moment, explaining that the "unknown god" was, in fact, the God of the Bible.

In Japan, too, many people may be worshipping an "unknown god." They may think they're praying to Buddhist figures or Shinto deities, but the blessings they receive may actually come from the God of Scripture.

Shandao and the Influence of Nestorian Christianity

Nestorian Christianity—known in East Asia as Jingjiao—came from the West and had a surprisingly deep impact on China, especially on Chinese Buddhism.
One key figure to look at is Shandao (613–681), a major proponent of Pure Land Buddhism during the Tang Dynasty. His teachings later inspired Japanese monks like Genshin and Hōnen, and Hōnen's disciple was none other than Shinran, the founder of Jōdo Shinshū.

What's fascinating is that Shandao himself seems to have been significantly influenced by Nestorian Christianity. In 635, Nestorian missionaries received official permission from Emperor Taizong to preach in China, and they began spreading their message widely. They taught that "everyone who calls on the name of the Lord will be saved" (Romans 10:13), encouraging people to say things like "I believe in Jesus," "I rely on Jesus," or "I entrust myself to Jesus." In Buddhist terms, this would be expressed as Namu Iesu-sama—"I take refuge in Jesus."

Shandao, who was living in the capital city of Chang'an at the time, likely heard these teachings. Later, he developed the practice of chanting Namu Amida Butsu—"I take refuge in Amitābha Buddha"—a six-syllable phrase that became central to Pure Land Buddhism. While belief in Amitābha had already existed in India, influenced by the Apostle Thomas, Shandao simplified the practice into this powerful mantra. He taught that simply chanting the name could lead to salvation—a concept that closely mirrors the biblical idea that calling on the Lord's name brings redemption.

So, Buddhism didn't evolve in isolation within Asia. It was shaped by encounters with Western religious thought, leading to profound transformations. When we understand this background, we begin to see that the mystical elements of Mahāyāna Buddhism and the devotion to Amitābha aren't just internal developments—they're the result of dynamic exchanges with other spiritual traditions.

The Arrival of Western Religions During the Tang Dynasty

Next, let's take a closer look at the religious exchanges that unfolded in China during the Tang Dynasty. This was a time when a wide variety of religions from the West began flowing into mainland China. Among them, three stood out for their lasting impact: Zoroastrianism (Xianjiao), Nestorian Christianity (Jingjiao), and Manichaeism (Mingjiao). These three were later collectively referred to as the "Three Foreign Religions of the Tang Dynasty" because of how deeply they influenced Chinese religious culture.

Zoroastrianism had already arrived during the earlier Northern and Southern Dynasties, but it was during the Tang era that Nestorianism and Manichaeism entered the scene. Thanks to the Tang Dynasty's open-minded governance, these religions flourished—especially in cosmopolitan cities like Chang'an. At the time, Chang'an was a bustling metropolis with over a million residents, a melting pot of languages, customs, and cultures. The streets were alive with magicians, dancers, musicians, and performers from all over the world.

However, as time went on, political tides shifted. Under Emperor Wuzong's anti-Buddhist campaign known as the "Huichang Suppression of Buddhism," many foreign religions—including these three—faced heavy persecution and decline.

Still, the religious dynamics of the Tang Dynasty played a major role in shaping the cultural landscape of East Asia. The ideas, rituals, and ceremonial structures introduced by these foreign faiths didn't vanish—they were absorbed, adapted, and eventually became part of the traditional cultures of countries like Japan and others across the region.

The Lost Ten Tribes of Israel and Their Journey Along the Silk Road

Now we're entering a slightly more unusual topic. Many Jewish scholars and historians believe that after the northern kingdom of ancient Israel was conquered by Assyria, the Ten Lost Tribes were scattered across the world. One theory suggests that as they moved eastward—through Afghanistan, Pakistan, Central Asia, and eventually into India and China—they preserved their unique customs and beliefs. Some even propose that these tribes eventually reached Japan.

Interestingly, traditions passed down among these groups include practices like levirate marriage (where a brother marries his deceased brother's widow) and ancient rituals that differ from mainstream Judaism. Some researchers have pointed out similarities between these customs and certain Japanese festivals—such as the Onbashira and Okami rituals at Suwa Taisha Shrine. These ceremonies reflect themes of absolute trust in divine power and mystical intervention, much like the biblical story of Abraham preparing to sacrifice his son Isaac.

Along the Silk Road, there are ethnic groups believed to be descendants of the Ten Tribes—such as the Pashtuns, certain communities in northern India and Myanmar, and the Qiang and Chang-Min peoples in China's Sichuan Province. These groups have been noted for preserving customs that resemble ancient Israelite traditions. Some even refer to themselves as "Children of Israel" and maintain rituals and beliefs that echo Jewish practices and biblical themes.
Their existence suggests a surprising and long-forgotten connection between Israel and the East—one that may have quietly shaped cultural and spiritual traditions across Asia.

The Origins of the Japanese People and Genetic Evidence

Now let's turn to the origins of the Japanese people. Modern genetic research shows that the Japanese population is made up of three major ancestral groups: the Jōmon people, the Yayoi people, and the Yamato ethnic group. To break it down:
- About 50% of modern Japanese belong to haplogroup O, which is linked to the Yayoi people who migrated from the Chinese mainland and the Korean Peninsula, bringing rice cultivation with them.

- Around 35–40% belong to haplogroup D, which is unique to Japan and associated with the Yamato people.
- The remaining 10% fall under haplogroup C, connected to the indigenous Jōmon people.

What's especially intriguing is haplogroup D. Globally, it's quite rare, and in Japan, it's most commonly found among the Yamato people, particularly in the Nara region. Some studies suggest that this D lineage may be closely related to the DE lineage found among ancient Israelites. This raises the possibility that the Yamato people and ancient Israelites might share not only genetic ties but cultural ones as well.

There's even a theory that certain Israelite tribes—like the tribe of Ephraim—were regarded as sacred lineages, and that Japan's imperial family may descend from this D lineage. These ideas have fueled long-standing discussions around the "Japan-Israel common ancestry theory" or the "Japan-Israel kinship theory."

Beyond genetics, physical cultural traits also reflect differences among the Jōmon, Yayoi, and Yamato groups. For example, tattooing was practiced by both the Jōmon and Yayoi peoples, but this tradition contrasts with ancient Israelite values, where tattoos were forbidden in the Bible. This distinction highlights how the Yamato culture, often seen as sacred, stood apart from neighboring traditions.

Parallels Between Japanese Traditions and Ancient Israelite Rituals

Now we're getting to one of the most fascinating parts of this whole story. Many of the rituals, traditions, and structures found in Japan's Shinto shrines bear striking similarities to the religious practices of ancient Israel.

Take the Ontōsai festival at Suwa Taisha, for example. It closely resembles the biblical story of Abraham preparing to sacrifice his son Isaac at God's command. In the Bible, Abraham travels to the land of Moriah, where a lamb is miraculously provided as a substitute offering. The altar and ceremonial hall used in the Ontōsai—called the Jikkendō—are reminiscent of the Tabernacle of Moses or even the Temple in Jerusalem. During the ritual, a young boy undergoes a symbolic moment of suffering, evoking the emotional depth of biblical sacrifice.

Then there's the grand Onbashira festival, held every seven years. Massive logs are cut, transported with solemn reverence, and erected as sacred pillars—symbolizing the divine seat or presence. This practice echoes the ancient Israelite tradition of constructing altars with symbolic pillars. Even the layout of Shinto shrines—with a worship hall in front, a main sanctuary behind, and a deeply protected sacred space at the very back—mirrors the structure of the biblical Tabernacle and the Holy of Holies.

The attire of Shinto priests is also worth noting. Their white linen robes with tassels on the sleeves are strikingly similar to the garments worn by Israelite priests. In the Bible, priests were commanded to wear white and attach tassels as part of their sacred duties. Likewise, Japanese priests don pure white robes during solemn ceremonies, preserving this tradition to this day.

Even the physical features of shrines—like the torii gates, offering boxes, and shimenawa ropes dividing sacred and secular spaces—share common ground with ancient Israelite temple design. The torii, in particular, resemble the two pillars described at the entrance of Israelite temples. Some scholars even draw parallels between the red accents on torii gates and the biblical account of lamb's blood marking doorposts on the eve of the Exodus.

And finally, rituals like purification at the temizuya (water basin), the act of clapping during prayer, and the concept of spiritual cleansing all echo practices found in ancient Israelite worship. The similarities in form and function are so precise, it's hard to dismiss them as mere coincidence.

Connections Between Japanese New Year Traditions and Ancient Israelite Rituals

Let's now turn our attention to Japanese New Year customs and other seasonal traditions. As many people know, it's customary in Japan to do a thorough house cleaning before the New Year—cleansing both the home and the body to prepare for a fresh start. Interestingly, this practice closely resembles the biblical Feast of Unleavened Bread, where the Israelites removed all leaven from their homes as a symbol of purification, as described in the Book of Exodus.

Other New Year traditions, like eating nanakusa-gayu (seven-herb rice porridge), visiting shrines on New Year's Day (hatsumōde), decorating with narase mochi during Koshōgatsu (Little New Year), and the ritual of mochi-tsuki (rice cake pounding), are thought to echo the Israelites' remembrance of manna—the miraculous food provided by God during their journey through the wilderness. These customs may not just be seasonal or folkloric—they could be unconscious echoes of ancestral experiences rooted in hardship and divine intervention.

Even decorations like kadomatsu (pine gate ornaments), shimenawa (sacred ropes), and the way holidays are scheduled throughout the year show surprising parallels with ancient Israelite laws and ceremonial structures. Some researchers suggest that these similarities point to a shared cultural memory that has evolved naturally over thousands of years.

Taken together, these traditions offer a fascinating glimpse into the possibility that Japanese customs and ancient Israelite practices may be more connected than we've ever imagined—woven together through time, migration, and spiritual resonance.

The Historical Development and Significance of the Japan–Israel Common Ancestry Theory

Now, based on everything we've explored so far, the idea that the Ten Lost Tribes of ancient Israel—and other descendants of the Jewish people—traveled eastward via the Silk Road and eventually settled in Japan isn't just a fanciful theory. In fact, it's supported by a growing body of historical evidence that suggests this "Ancient Israelite Migration Theory" or "Japan–Israel Common Ancestry Theory" may have real substance.

Over the years, many researchers have supported this view. In the early Meiji era, N. McLeod from Scotland, Professor Edward F. Odlum, and Dr. M. Spielman from South Africa all argued that traces of ancient Israelite heritage could be found among the Japanese people. The Jewish Encyclopedia even mentions this theory, and Jewish scholars who lived and studied in Japan have reported similarities between ancient Israelite traditions and Japanese imperial customs and rituals.

Notably, Takatoshi Kobayashi (a grandson of Emperor Meiji) and Kaoru Nakamaru have pointed to evidence of connections between the Japanese imperial family and Judaism. They claim that Emperor Meiji once said, "Japan is Shinto, but Shinto originally comes from Judaism," and that symbols like the Star of David and practices like circumcision exist within the imperial household. The formal name of Emperor Jimmu—Kamu-Yamato-Iware-Biko-Sumeramikoto—has also been interpreted by some as containing phonetic elements derived from Hebrew, suggesting a link to ancient Jewish royalty.
Scholars like Naohiko Nakajima have proposed that Emperor Jimmu descended from the southern kingdom of Judah, while others like Aidelberg associate him with the dispersed tribes of northern Israel. These interpretations blur the line between historical record and legend, but they open up intriguing possibilities about cultural exchange and hidden origins within the Japanese imperial lineage.

Importantly, this theory doesn't claim that "Japanese people are simply Jewish." Rather, it emphasizes that the Japanese are a diverse mix of peoples—including migrants from the Korean Peninsula, Sakhalin, and Southeast Asia—but that at the core of this mix, there may be a strong influence from ancient Israelites who journeyed eastward. In this view, the Yamato people—and possibly the imperial family—could be deeply connected to Israel through both blood and tradition.
Historically, this theory gained attention during the Meiji period as Japan faced pressure from Western powers. It was partly a way to reclaim pride and identity. But today, the conversation has shifted. It's no longer just about national self-esteem—it's about interdisciplinary research, historical i inquiry, and the search for objective evidence.

Conclusion and Future Outlook

We've covered a lot—Buddhism's transformation, the arrival of Western religions in China, the journey of the Lost Ten Tribes along the Silk Road, the genetic makeup of the Japanese people, and the striking similarities between Shinto rituals and ancient Israelite traditions. At first glance, these topics may seem scattered across different times and places. But when you look closely, you begin to see how the echoes of people from distant lands have quietly shaped our culture—through sound, form, and ritual.

From the unique D haplogroup found in Japan's imperial lineage, to the architecture of Shinto shrines, priestly garments, and even New Year customs—none of these elements appear to be mere coincidence. They're the result of centuries of migration, cultural exchange, and spiritual convergence. These layers of evidence offer us powerful clues for understanding the shared threads of human history—beyond borders and ethnic divisions. And they open the door to exciting new discoveries in fields like history, genetics, religious studies, and folklore.

This journey of connecting past and present through culture, faith, and science isn't just academic—it's a meaningful opportunity for people to reflect on their roots and identity. If Japan and ancient Israel truly share a deep connection, then behind that lies a grand story of humanity: one of long journeys, encounters between civilizations, and mutual influence that helped shape the world we live in today.

And finally, let's touch on the topic of the "End Times." According to biblical prophecy, the end of the world will usher in a new divine order. Signs of this include the restoration of Israel, the building of a Third Temple, and the spread of the Gospel across the globe. Events like wars, earthquakes, famine, and the growing coldness in human hearts are seen as precursors to this final chapter.
The Gospel of Matthew, chapter 24, records Jesus speaking to his disciples:

"Watch out that no one deceives you. For many will come in my name, claiming, 'I am the Messiah,' and will deceive many. You will hear of wars and rumors of wars... Nation will rise against nation, and kingdom against kingdom. There will be famines and earthquakes in various places... All these are the beginning of birth pains... But the one who stands firm to the end will be saved. And this gospel of the kingdom will be preached in the whole world... and then the end will come."

The Book of Revelation also describes the "Seven Trumpets," which bring disasters like fire, cosmic disturbances, and meteor strikes. Later, demonic forces emerge, and a vast army—said to number 200 million—rises from the East to strike humanity. During this time, two prophets sent by God will appear, delivering His message for three and a half years. Though they will be struck down, they will rise again—marking a dramatic turning point in the prophetic narrative.

And Then the Final Trumpet Will Sound

According to biblical prophecy, when the final trumpet sounds, a figure known as the Antichrist will rise—a global dictator who ushers in the battle of Armageddon. This marks the beginning of Christ's Second Coming, the resurrection of the dead, and the rapture of believers. At that point, God's glorious Millennial Kingdom will be established on Earth. The old world will be renewed into a new heaven and a new earth, and this transformation is said to include the restoration of the Ten Lost Tribes and a spiritual awakening in Japan.

One prophecy worth highlighting is found in Ezekiel 37—the vision of the "dry bones." Ezekiel sees a valley filled with lifeless bones, seemingly abandoned and without hope. But when God commands him to prophesy, and His breath enters the bones, they begin to reconnect—sinews form, flesh appears, and the bones rise up as a vast, living army. It's a powerful symbol of spiritual revival: no matter how lifeless or forgotten something may seem, when God breathes life into it, restoration is possible.

Looking at Japan today, the number of churches and Christians is still quite small. Yet prophecy suggests that as the end times approach, the glory of God will also rise from the East. In this light, the vision of the dry bones may reflect the spiritual state of Japan—where hearts that seem dormant or distant from faith could be revived by the breath of God, sparking a profound awakening.

Ultimately, I hope this discussion encourages us to reflect on the importance of cultural exchange and the deeper meanings behind it. The story we've explored—woven from history, science, tradition, and prophecy—is complex, beautiful, and still unfolding. May it continue to inspire new insights and discoveries as we move forward.

Closing Thoughts

What I've shared today is just one perspective among many. Of course, these ideas require further discussion and careful examination, and I fully recognize that much of my own research is still a work in progress. But even so, the possibility that ancient Israel and Japan may be deeply connected—through bloodlines, faith, traditions, and rituals—is profoundly moving. It reminds us of the rich, layered complexity of our culture and heritage.

This summary has touched on a wide range of topics: the influence between religions, the transmission of traditional customs, the genetic makeup of the Japanese people, and the striking similarities in ritual practices. Each of these areas deserves continued attention as part of interdisciplinary research. New discoveries in DNA analysis or folklore studies could shed fresh light on existing theories. And as we revisit the history of cultural exchange, these discussions offer meaningful insights that go far beyond academic interest.

I hope this exploration encourages you to reflect more deeply on your own roots and to engage with these themes in your own way—whether through study, conversation, or personal inquiry. The story of how cultures meet, merge, and evolve is not only fascinating—it's essential to understanding who we are and how we've come to be.

Israel in Japan

By Hideo Hatakeda

神輿 portable shrine

(MIKOSHI = ARK)

Photo 1 Matsuo Taisha Mikoshi

Festivals are popular at shrines that practice Shinto, the Japanese religion. At these festivals, a mikoshi (portable shrine) is always carried. What does that mean? I'll tell you about it later. Its size, gold plating, the pole attached to the base, and the phoenix, a mythical bird considered an angel or cherub, with its wings spread at the top make it a truly special sight. This is the mikoshi of Matsuo Taisha Shrine.

Photo 2 Gion festival (Mikoshi at the Kyoto Gion Festival, Yasaka Shrine)

Mikoshi (ark) The portable shrine used in the festival at Matsuo Shrine, a shrine with a long tradition in Kyoto, features beautifully curved wings pointing skyward, symbolizing the cherubim described in the Bible. (See Photo 1.) The Ark of the Covenant and the portable shrine are identical in both meaning and shape.

Then, thunder really struck. The sounds were so similar that I remembered passages in the Old and New Testaments about how it was impossible to distinguish between the sound of thunder and the voice of God. This shrine has a legend about the miracle of water turning into sake.

Photo 3 Mikoshi entering the river

The Ark of the Covenant in Israel was also carried by the Levites. Historic Japanese mikoshi are also carried only by a select few. Furthermore, the mikoshi of Kyoto's Matsuo Taisha Shrine enters the Katsura River, as if to commemorate the time when the Ark of the Covenant crossed the Jordan River.

Kono Shrine, located near Amanohashidate on the Tango Peninsula in Kyoto, is said to be the original Ise shrine, and is home to Ise's Outer Shrine, Manai Shrine, which is in charge of meals. The shrine's symbol is the Kagome crest. Surprisingly, that symbol is the Star of David. A short distance north along the coastline, near the Ine boathouses, Yasaka Shrine's portable shrine (mikoshi) enters the sea in July. Young people perform a ceremony to pull it back up to shore.

I heard this from someone who has carried a portable shrine in the Tohoku region. "The mikoshi doesn't sink, even though its feet don't touch the riverbed," they wondered. It's not that the mikoshi doesn't sink because it's light. It is gold-plated inside and out and decorated with various ornaments. "It is so heavy that it will never float in water."

All over Japan, portable shrines are carried into rivers, and the reason for this is said to be as a festival to remember when the Ark of the Covenant of Israel crossed the Jordan River. (Photo 3) When carrying a mikoshi (portable shrine) at Japanese festivals, the carriers chant "Essa, essa." While the meaning of this chant is unclear in Japanese, Eli Cohen, Israel's ambassador to Japan for three years until 2007, said on a December 2005 television program that "essa" in Hebrew means to carry, or "carry" in English. After a lecture as part of the Bible and Japan Forum, I asked in the car, "What is the Hebrew word for the Ark of the Covenant, which closely resembles the Japanese mikoshi (portable shrine)?" The answer was, "Mikadashi." There are said to be as many as 35,000 mikoshi in Japan. Are they replicas? They represent the culmination of efforts to preserve the national identity of the ancient Israelites, who inherited the Ark of the Covenant and passed on God's covenant to future generations.

The Old Testament (Exodus 25) mentions a sacred object called the "Ark of the Covenant." It was made of acacia wood, two and a half cubits long, one and a half cubits wide, and one and a half cubits high, approximately 120cm x 70cm x 70cm. It was overlaid inside and out with pure gold. Four gold rings were made for the Ark, each attached to the base of its four corners. Two rings were attached to one side and two to the other. Poles were made of acacia wood, overlaid with gold, and passed through the rings on each side of the Ark so that it could be carried. The poles were to remain inserted into the rings and never be removed. Also above the Ark were two hammered golden cherubim (angels). They had their wings stretched out upward, covering the mercy cover with their wings, facing each other. No one was allowed to touch the Ark.

3,000 years ago, King David of Israel said, "No one may carry the Ark of God except the Levites, for God has chosen them to serve him." He also told the Levites who carried the Ark, "Consecrate yourselves and bring up the Ark of the Lord, the God of Israel, to the place I have designated for it." They were to purify themselves before the Ark of the Covenant. They sang before the Ark and played harps, psalters, tambourines, castanets, and cymbals, and danced with all their might for joy before the Lord.

King David stripped off his royal garments, put on a linen cloth over his undergarments, and danced nearly naked before the Ark of the Lord, sounding trumpets. After the Ark of the Covenant was placed in its designated place, each man and woman was given a loaf of bread, a date cake, and a raspberry cake.

Just before the people of Israel were delivered from slavery in Egypt and were about to enter the Promised Land, they experienced a great miracle. They reached the banks of the Jordan River, the final hurdle before entering the Promised Land, a land flowing with milk and honey. During harvest, the Jordan River overflows its banks. But when the Levites leading the way carrying the Ark of the Covenant dipped their feet into the water's edge, the waters flowing down from above rose to a spurt. The waters formed a dam, blocking the way, and the people crossed in front of Jericho. Joshua was the leader of the Israelites, and with armed soldiers at the front, the Ark of the Covenant followed, and the priests blew the trumpets, they carried the Ark around the walls of Jericho, causing the walls to collapse.

The Bible also records the following story about the Ark of the Covenant: When the Ark was taken from Israel, disaster struck the land. When it was placed in the Philistine temple of Dagon, Dagon's head and arms were cut off before the Ark of the Lord. The people of that area were stricken with boils. So they moved it to Gath in fear, where a great panic struck the area, and they too were stricken with boils. So they moved it to Ekron, where the people of Ekron trembled in fear of death, saying, "Are you turning away the Ark of the God of Israel to kill us?" It is recorded that 57,000 people died when the people of Beth-shemesh saw inside the Ark.

After several changes, the Ark was placed in the temple of the Lord. During David's time, it was temporarily moved from Baalah to David's own city, the City of David, where it ceased to ascend, but was brought up again to David's own city. When King Solomon built the temple, it was placed there. What was inside the Ark? Let's quote from 2 Chronicles chapter 5, verse 7:

"The priests brought the ark of the Lord's covenant into its place, into the Most Holy Place, the inner sanctum of the temple, under the wings of the cherubim. Its poles were long, so that their ends were visible from the Holy Place in front of the inner sanctuary, but not from outside. There was nothing inside the ark except the two tablets."

When it was first made, the ark contained Aaron's rod, a jar of manna, and the two stone tablets of the Ten Commandments. These were the three sacred treasures of Israel. Where did the other two sacred treasures go?

Shrine structure

Who designed the shrine's structure and spread it throughout the country? A structure very similar to it is recorded in the Bible. Going back several hundred years into Japanese history, between 1275 and 1235 BC, the Israelites escaped from Egypt led by Moses and wandered the wilderness. At that time, they built a tabernacle where God was said to be present. The design is so similar that it is hard to imagine that the blueprints for this shrine were used to build it. It is 100 cubits long (1 cubit is

45 cm, so 45 meters), and 50 cubits wide (22 meters). The length to width ratio is 2:1. It is surrounded by linen cloth hung on 80 sturdy pillars.

The gates were 20 cubits (9 meters) wide and made of blue, purple, and scarlet twisted linen, and were supported by four pillars and bronze bases. The inside of the tabernacle was divided into two sections: the Holy Place in the front and the Most Holy Place in the back. The Holy Place and the Most Holy Place were separated by a cloth, and in the center of the Most Holy Place was placed the Ark of the Covenant, covered in gold.

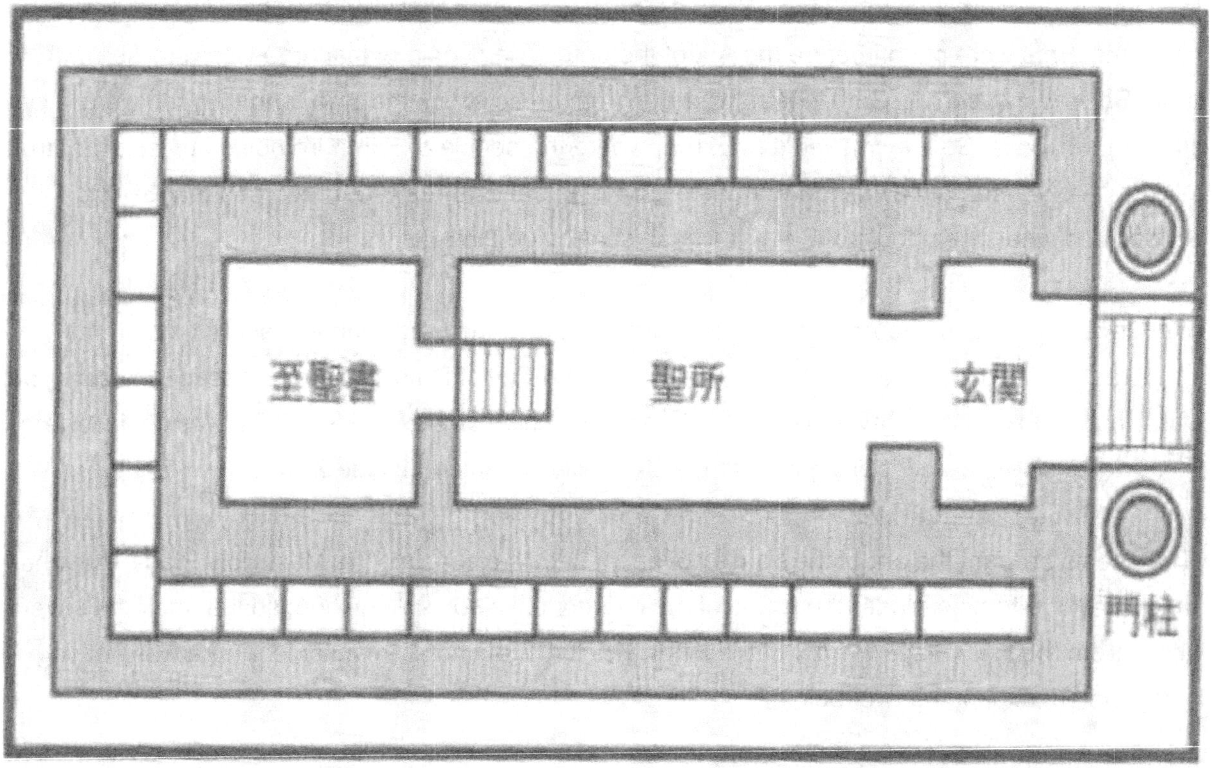

Temple of Solomon

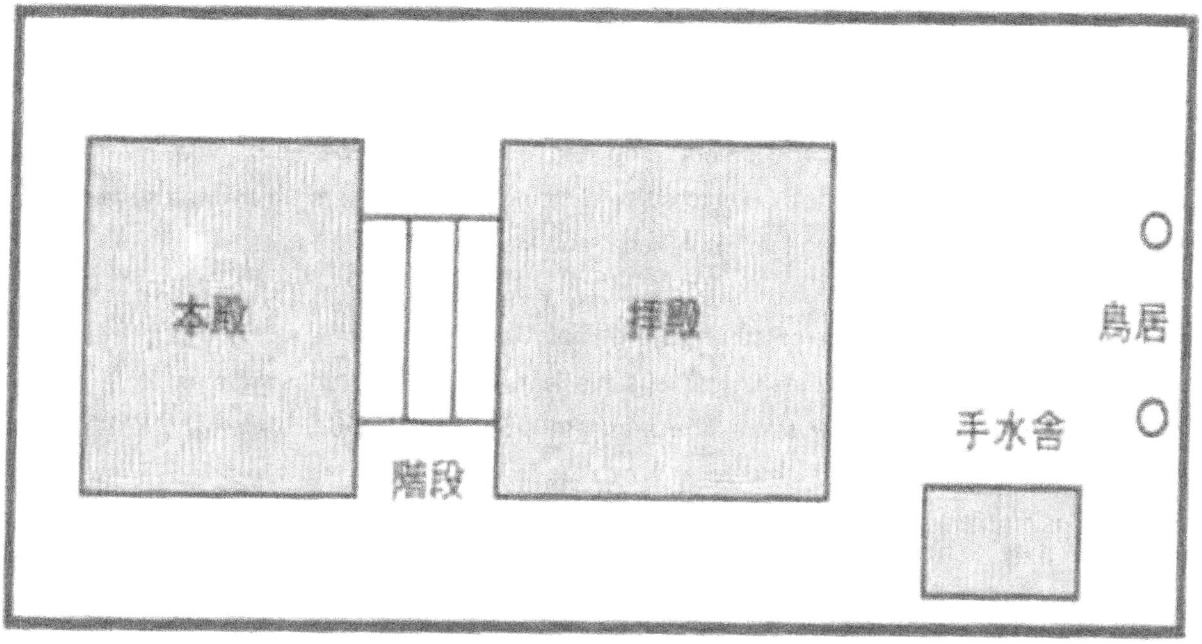

Temple “Jinja”

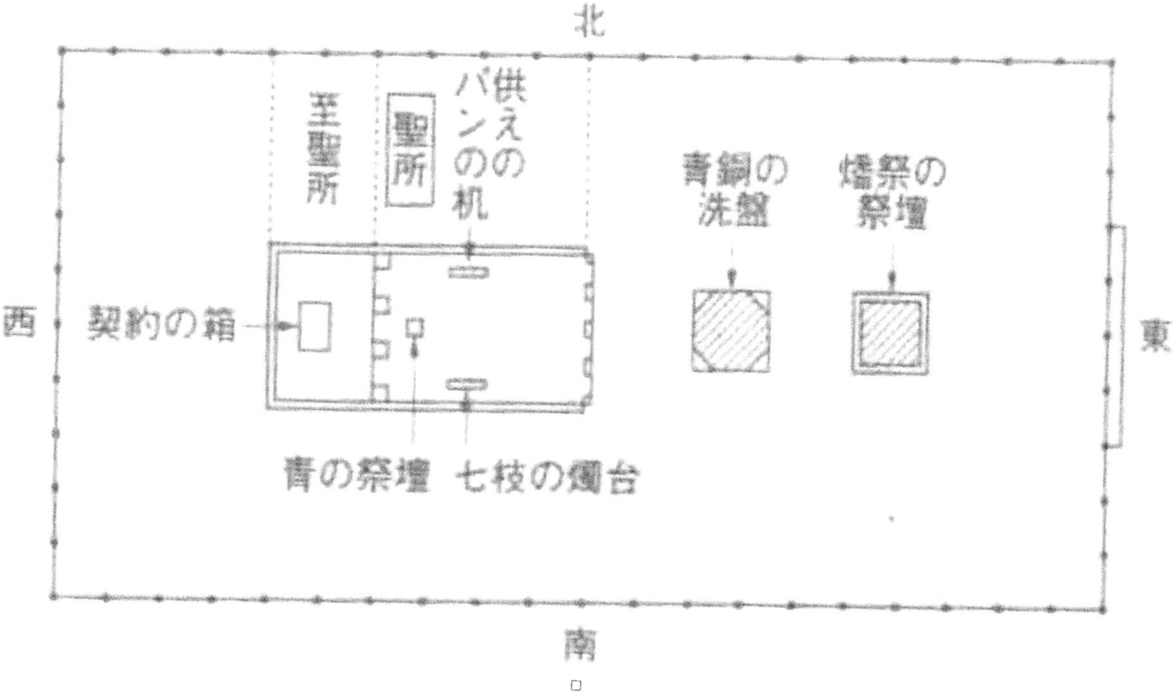

Japanese shrine

Temple of Solomon

Only the priests could enter the Holy Place. The innermost Holy of Holies was entered only once a year, on Yom Kippur (the Day of Atonement). The innermost Holy of Holies in Solomon's Temple was located on a higher level and could be entered by climbing a flight of stairs. There was a staircase about three meters wide between the "Holy Place" and the "Most Holy of Holies."

Similarly, at the Japanese shrine of Ise Jingu, the "main hall" at the back is slightly higher than the "haiden" at the front, and has 12 steps. Perhaps this represents the 12 tribes. In Israel, only the high priest can go to the bottom of the stairs. The Japanese emperor is called "His Majesty." This means "below the stairs." The Japanese emperor is not called Emperor in English. It is called "Priest King," which means high priest.

Judaism abolishes idols and detests them. That's why there are no idols in the temple. It was also built facing east, as the glory of God was revealed from the east.

Now, let's look at the structure of Japanese shrines. Solomon's Temple was magnificent, but it cannot be called a shrine in itself. However, if it is based on the tabernacle, its length and width are two to one, and the worship hall and main hall are also the sanctuary and the holiest of places, and the purpose and spatial layout are the same. The structure of Ise Shrine is immediately clear from the second floor of the nearby Chokokan, where you can see Ise Shrine from directly above. People call shrines "Yashiro." The simple structure of a Yashiro is two pillars at the entrance. This is called a Torii (gate). It is the boundary between the secular world and the sacred world (spiritual world), which can also be called the sacred precincts. When people enter this gate, they forget about the secular world and enter a garden called the Keidai (precincts). The central structure is the place of worship, which has a dual structure consisting of a worship hall (haiden) and a main hall (honden), which are separate buildings. Anyone can enter the worship hall, but only priests can enter the main hall a few times a year, and only on special occasions such as festivals and ceremonies. There are 12 steps between the worship hall and the main hall.

On either side of the entrance to the shrine's worship hall are a lion and a pair of guardian lions (Shishi the Lion and Komainu the unicorn with horns on its head). Both of them lions, which do not exist in Japan, are enshrined here as if to guard the temple.

Shimogamo Jinja in Kyoto

A similar pair of animals is enshrined in the temple in Israel. The lion in Israel symbolizes the tribe of Judah, head of the two southern tribes of Israel, and the guardian lion (unicorn) symbolizes Ephraim, head of the ten northern tribes of Israel. Neither the lions nor the guardian lions at shrines are worshiped as idols.

There is also a mirror placed there, but this is not worshipped as an idol. Shinto gods are invisible deities, and idols are not found in shrines. Most shrines face east. Ancient styles include Shinmei-zukuri, Taisha-zukuri, and Sumiyoshi-zukuri, and are simple, using straight lines.

Mount Moriah in Japan...

Suwa's Ontosai and the God of Abraham and Isaac

Located in the center of Japan

Ontosai

Mt. Moriya

This solemn festival is conducted without dancing or shouting, and all the men in attendance are dressed in formal suits. This ritual is of immense importance. It takes place every year on April 15th at the Kamisha Maemiya of Suwa Taisha Shrine, approximately 7 kilometers south of Lake Suwa in Chino City. Mount Moriah (1,631.2 meters), the inner sanctuary and sacred object of worship, lies behind the Maemiya, a mountain often described as the center of Honshu. The view from its summit offers a magnificent 360-degree panorama. The Moriya family, which has worshiped the shrine's main deity, Mishakuchi, for 78 generations, serves as the chief priest.

Mishakuchi-no-Kami (god of Misakuchi)

The M in M-ISAKU-CHI is thought to be a prefix consonant, while Isaac and CHI are suffixes. Some also suggest it is an archaic word for snake. It has been written in kanji「御佐口神」「三社口神」「御社宮司神」「佐久神」「射軍神」「尺神」as "Misakuchi-no-Kami," "Sansha-guchi-no-Kami," "Misha-guji-no-Kami," "Saku-no-Kami," "Igun-no-Kami," or "Shaku-no-Kami," but there is no consensus. All of these are ateji (phonetic spellings) and are originally foreign words. Let's compare the "Oko-ikenie" ritual (divine sacrifice) of the Edo period Ontou (one head) Festival, copied by the mid-Edo period scholar and travel writer Sugae Masumi, with Genesis 22 in the Old Testament.

Records by Sugae Masumi

I walked about 16 cho (approximately 170 m) east from here. In a place called Maemiya, there was a Naoraiden hall with a 10-ken (18 meters) entrance. There, 75 deer heads were lined up on a wooden board. Among them was a deer with a torn ear. It was said that this deer had been caught by a god with a spear. ...Soon, the chief priest rose from his position and went under a tree. He had a bow and arrow in hand, and it seemed as if he was about to shoot something. ...Eventually, he untied the bundle of reeds, took pieces of reeds, laid them on top, and added flowers. The head of the shrine remains motionless. Then, a pointed pillar about five feet (1.5 meters) long and five inches (1.5 centimeters) wide is pushed up. This is called an otsue (sacred staff) or an oniebashira (sacrificial pillar), but what is the difference? ...A child around eight years old, called the Okou (god), dressed in a crimson kimono, places his hands on the pillar. The people join forces to push the pillar up onto the bamboo mat. Then, a man in full attire takes out a wisteria sword from a small brocade bag, draws it, and hands it to the head of the shrine. ...Then, after three claps, the kagura dance stops. The god's child is then tied up with a rope made of twisted mulberry bark. As the rope is tied, the people simply call out, "Mazu. Mazu." (Fairly good) A torch is lit. ...The festival reaches its climax. A horse carrying an emissary from the governor of Suwa Province appears. People throw things at the horse's head. However, the horse runs very fast. A large group of children then chases after the horse. Afterwards, a priest carrying the sacrificial pillar on his shoulder shouts, "Treasure! Treasure!" He places five long bell-like objects in a brocade bag, hangs them on a tree branch, and slowly runs off, making seven large circles around the shrine's front yard before disappearing. Then, in the front yard of the Nagaden hall, the child who had been tied with the bark of a mulberry tree is released, and the festival comes to an end. (From Sugae Masumi's Shinano Journey, Shinkyo Publishing)

The Current "Ontou Festival" (head festival)

While the custom of the "Oniebashira" (offering pillar) remains, the "Oko" ritual is no longer performed. Taxidermy is used. Until the Meiji period, 75 deer heads were reportedly offered. A priest reverently holds a stuffed head behind a curtain stretched around the Jukkenro corridor of the Maemiya Shrine. The centerpiece of the offerings, accompanied by the sounds of gagaku music, is, of course, a child named "Oko." However, the child is no longer present. On April 15th, when this ritual, which may have spanned two thousand years, was taking place, the Jukkenro corridor would have been crimson red with the blood of the animals. The Suwa Taisha Kamisha Shrine stands out nationwide for its bloody animal sacrifice rituals, says Kaifu, the chief priest of Kono Shrine on the Tango Peninsula in Kyoto, describing it as a mysterious festival in Japan.

This is precisely because it is an exception within Shinto. Fujimori Terunobu writes, "It is full of mystery. Why push the child, the deity, up the mountain along with the sacrificial pillar and then tie him to a tree?" In 1871 (Meiji 4th year), the new government banned this festival, citing it as human sacrifice. When I asked the priest officiating the festival, "Isn't this a ritual that misses the most important part?" he replied, "Yes. It's unfortunate. It's truly regrettable that we are unable to protect the most important part. They are trying to kill the child with a rattan sword, and we are stepping in to stop them, so we are teaching that this is not a Hitomi Goku (human sacrifice) so to say that this gesture is wrong is a misunderstanding."

What is the significance of sacrificing a single child?

The main character of this festival is a young boy who represents the deity (Okou), a great celebration priest. He begins by making a pilgrimage in three directions around the town of Chino City. In particular, for the outer ritual of the pilgrimage, he departs three days in advance. The three days before that are related to Abraham.

Genesis 22: Abraham's Trial

God put Abraham to the test. He said, "Take your son, your only son Isaac, whom you love, and go to the land of Moriah. Offer him up as a burnt offering on one of the mountains I will tell you about." Early the next morning, Abraham saddled his donkey and took two of his young men and his son Isaac with him. On the third day, Abraham looked up and saw the place in the distance. ... He took the wood for the burnt offering and placed it on his son Isaac. He took the fire and the knife in his hand, and they went on together. ... They arrived at the place God had told him about, and Abraham built an altar there. He arranged the wood, bound his son Isaac, and laid him on the altar, on top of the wood. Abraham reached out his hand and took a knife to slay his son, but an angel of the Lord called to him from heaven, "Abraham, Abraham!" He said, "Do not put your hand on the boy, or do anything to him. Now I know that you fear God, for you have not withheld your son, your only son, from me." Abraham lifted up his eyes and looked, and behold, a ram caught in a thicket by its horns. Abraham went and took the ram and offered it as a burnt offering instead of his son. So Abraham named that place Adonai-Ireh. To this day it is said, "It will be provided on the mount of the Lord." The story doesn't end there. Immediately afterward, God made great promises to Abraham and his descendants. These promises were passed down to Isaac, his son Jacob, and Jacob, who was renamed Israel and became the father of the twelve tribes. They also produced David and Solomon, and the prosperity of that time was unparalleled in the world. And the power that had such a profound mental and spiritual impact on the whole world continues to this day, becoming a source of blessing for the entire world. This promise cannot be overlooked.

"I swear by myself, because you have done this and have not withheld your son, your only son, I will surely bless you and make your descendants as numerous as the stars of the sky and the sand of the sea. And your descendants will possess the gates of their enemies. And in your descendants all nations of the earth will be blessed, because you have obeyed my voice."

I've quoted a long passage from the Bible, but I just can't leave this out. Because it leads to David, the 14th generation from Abraham, and Jesus, the 14th generation born from David as the Savior, being sacrificed on the cross for the sins of mankind.

The story of Abraham's blessing is unfamiliar to us Japanese, even though he is an important figure not only in Christian-based Western countries but also in Islamic-based Islamic countries. However, if the Ontou (Head) Festival, which has been handed down at Suwa Taisha Shrine, one of the origins of divine faith, is the sacred ritual of the offering of Isaac that has been carried out since the founding of Japan, then this is a significant event. This means that Japan is a country that receives the blessing of Abraham. This is not just one of Japan's heritage sites, but a World Heritage Site. As we examine the striking similarities in the Ontou Festival one by one, we see that it is a traditional tale that puts the life of Abraham and his only son on the line. It has been preserved in our country as a solemn festival to remind us of the origins of our nation. This is one of the valuable pieces of evidence that the Northern Israelites came to and settled on the island nation of Japan, but I would like to point out one more similarity.

Three days had passed since Abraham heard God's voice, and he arrived at Mount Moriah. The festival began three days in advance, riding on horseback. Abraham tied up his only son and placed him on the wood. He swung the sword to slaughter Isaac. The "god (Okou the child)" was also tied up and pushed up onto a bamboo mat. The priest was about to swing his "rattan sword." At that very moment, God stopped Abraham's hand through an "angel." The Ontou Festival is described as the appearance of messengers on horseback and priests carrying sacrificial poles on their shoulders, and the child is released. While the Old Testament describes a ram caught in a bush by its horns as a sacrifice, this version describes 75 antlered deer lined up on a chopping block. Since sheep were not available in Japan, deer were likely used instead. One of them is special and called the ear-hugging deer, and is prepared by God. The number 75 heads comes from the fact that 75 sheep were slaughtered at the Passover in Samaria. The festival took place in Samaria, the capital of northern Israel, and on Mount Gerizim, which is Mount Moriah in Jerusalem in southern Israel. Mount Gerizim is also known as Mount Moriah for the people of northern Israel.

יחיד

Only one "ya'akoud" ← The kanji for "okou" is written as "on-kami (god)" or "kami no tsukai (the angel of God)," but this is a phonetic spelling. If you try to pronounce it phonetically, the "only son" in Genesis 22:2, "Isaac, the only son," is "ya'akoud" (meaning only one) in the original Hebrew.

Customs and Traditions

1. Salt
   For the Japanese, salt was not just a food, but also a tool for purification. A mound of salt called morijio (salt mound) was placed at the entrance of the house to purify the house. It was also customary to sprinkle salt on one's body before returning from a funeral and entering the house to purify oneself. The same goes for sprinkling salt before Sumo wrestling. Salt is an important offering to the gods, used to purify the shrine grounds, ritual implements, and household altars. Salt also has disinfectant properties and prevents food from corroding. This has been passed down in Japan's ancient Shinto religion and is even mentioned in the Bible (Leviticus 2:13). Rabbi Tokayer of Judaism said, "The custom of using salt on various occasions was practiced in both Japan and Judaism. The underlying philosophy of maintaining cleanliness is consistent in both countries. I think this is a very interesting similarity."

In the Sermon on the Mount, Jesus said, "You are the salt of the earth. But if the salt loses its saltiness, how can it be made salty? It is no longer good for anything but to be thrown out and trampled underfoot by men." Immediately after this sermon on salt, he said, "Do not think that I have come to abolish the Law or the Prophets. I have not come to abolish them, but to fulfill them." This shows that salt's original role is to purify, cleanse, and make people useful, and that salt holds the secret to making it natural for people to keep the commandments.

2. Taking Off Your Shoes
When a friend from New Zealand came to my house, he accidentally walked into his room with his shoes on through the entrance. In Japanese society, people take off their shoes when they return home. They also take off their shoes when they enter sacred places, such as the worship hall of a shrine. In ancient Israel, taking off one's shoes was a sacred command. When Moses met God and was given his calling to save his fellow Israelites, God told him, "Take off your shoes, for this is holy ground." When David was in dire straits, he climbed the Mount of Olives. This mountain is east of Jerusalem, 814 meters above sea level. It is the mountain where Jesus later prophesied the destruction of Jerusalem and where he stood when he ascended to heaven in front of his disciples after his resurrection. Whether he knew it or not, David took off his shoes and climbed barefoot to worship God. (2 Samuel 15:30)
3. Washing Your Feet
The custom of returning home, removing your shoes, and washing your feet has long been common in Japan. It's familiar to Japanese people and not something unusual. The Nihon Shoki, considered Japan's oldest book, tells of a man of noble appearance washing his feet at the entrance to a seaside house, signaling his recognition as the grandson of God.

The Bible tells of Jesus washing his disciple's feet, and the Master's washing of his disciple's feet indicates that forgiveness of sins is possible because Christ washes away the sins and impurities of everyday life. In the same way, it's important for us to forgive each other every day. For sinners, "washing their feet" represents becoming true human beings. Kyoto is home to the Tadasu-no-Mori Forest, a place where Shimogamo Shrine and the Silkworm Shrine are located. People would perform purification rituals there. There, a fresh spring water gushed forth from a pond. They would remove their shoes and clothing and immerse themselves in the water to purify their mind and body.

4. Clothing - Wearing an Obi
Japanese clothing is very similar to Jewish clothing. It's fair to say that the attire worn by Japanese samurai is similar to that worn by ancient princes in the Middle East.

Kimono and obi are inseparably linked. There is no kimono without an obi. It was a traditional custom in Japan to give an obi as a betrothal gift. As for the function of carrying tools (especially weapons), for example, a Japanese sword, a katana, is worn at the waist. In Japanese, the word "obiru" (to wear) means to be worn closest to the body. The same is true in Chinese characters; the word "obi" (to carry) already contains the character for "obi." Obi were important gifts given on important occasions. In the Bible, an obi appears to be one of the gifts given by David's soldier Joab to his subordinates as a reward. That's how important obi were. (2 Samuel 18:11) It is also recorded that Jonathan, David's dear friend and the son of the king at the time, gave David his armor and helmet, as well as his sword, bow, and belt. (1 Samuel 18:4)

Jesus also encouraged people to live their lives vigilantly and with faith in God, saying, "Keep your loins girded and your lamps burning." The importance of the belt is symbolically connected to the belt of the heart. Paul also said, "Love is the perfect binding belt," and Peter used the analogy of, "Therefore gird up the belt of your heart..."

A samurai is someone who wears a sword in his kimono and has a sense of mission that "to die is to live," which is part of the warrior's role of reviving and rising from the dead, as prophesied in biblical prophecy.

While swords are worn on the shoulders of Europeans and Chinese, the Japanese and ancient Israelites wore them tucked into their belts. The sword is not a tool of war used to pit people against each other, but it represents the word of God, which is powerful and sharper than any two-edged sword, piercing even to the division of soul and spirit, of joints and marrow, and is a discerner of the thoughts and intentions of the heart. The sword is a symbol of the prophetic word. He wears the sword in his belt.

Japan's Restoration

Japan-Israel Prophecy Fulfilled

Now, I would like to conclude. I will move on to prophecies for Japan and the Japanese people. Japan will be restored. The dry bones crouching in the valley will be resurrected. Japan's spirit has withered from its original state, and its spiritual strength has also withered. It is far from independent and unrestrained. Politically, there is no trace of Japan's former identity, and the strength that comes from its spirit of self-reliance and independence has been numbed by a Western sense of survival of the fittest. The bones that form the roots of its culture as a whole are thin, like osteoporosis, barely holding on, as if emaciated. And yet, the customs, habits, and traditions handed down from our ancestors truly live on in Japan.

The "remnants" (a biblical term meaning people who remain loyal and obey God even after various trials) of the lost ten tribes and the remaining two tribes are listening to biblical prophecies, praying, and beginning to prophesy in order to lift up Japan. This is where hope lies. The coming years will be a time when signs of recovery will become visible. I would like to record this ray of hope. The remaining handful of mainstream Northern Israelites who have arrived in Japan are moving toward the fulfillment of biblical prophecy, both ethnically and spiritually. Not only the Japanese people, but the world as a whole, are watching to find out what this prophecy is. This will be another year of great interest.

Japan is Ephraim, the mainstream of the Ten Lost Tribes. Ephraim is the name of Joseph's second son, whom he named after he was delivered from his suffering, saying, "God has made me fruitful in

the land of my affliction" (Genesis 41:52). He was the son of Joseph, Jacob's beloved son. Joseph's blessing was passed on to his sons, Ephraim and Manasseh. Leaving aside the details, the time has come for us Japanese to consider how Japan's future will unfold in the 21st century in light of the prophecies of Jacob and Moses to the tribe of Ephraim, discussed in the previous chapter.
Since it seems like the most common method to quote the Bible, which has been proven to be the most reliable prophecy in the history of the world, let's start next time with Romans 11, written by Paul, who wrote most of the New Testament.

"So has God rejected his people (Israel)? Absolutely not," it is prophesied, and Israel will be restored. If so, where is this Israel located in the 21st century? Is it the Israel of Palestine? That's half true. In 722 BC, Israel split into northern and southern Israel, and the northern part was destroyed by Assyria. In 586 BC, the southern part of Israel, part of the tribe of Judah, was taken captive in Babylon. Some of the southern Israelites later returned to their homeland, but by 70 AD, the southern part of Israel, part of the tribe of Judah, was completely destroyed by the Roman Empire, leaving the country in ruins and without mountains or rivers. All of Israel (the Bible refers to the entire house of Israel, all 12 tribes) was scattered throughout the world. This is what is known as the Diaspora.

History is a mysterious thing. Yet, in the mid-20th century, a portion of it was restored. A miracle, a wonder beyond compare, occurred. After 1900 years of wandering, on May 14, 1948, the Jews restored their homeland. If they had named it the Jewish Republic, it would have been easier to interpret Bible prophecy. However, they named it "Israel," believing that their brothers would also return in the future. Their hope and faith are admirable, but it is also true that it has led to misunderstandings. The brother to which their brothers would return is, of course, Northern Israel. The leader at that time was the tribe of Ephraim, and they were the ten lost tribes that had perished 2,700 years earlier. It is prophesied that their restoration would be such a miracle that cries of joy would reverberate throughout the whole world, causing the stories of the Israelites' escape from Egypt, their liberation, and their entry into the blessed land of Canaan to be forgotten. If the restoration of southern Israel, the Jewish people, to their homeland was a great miracle, then the restoration of all of Israel would be an even greater miracle. However, this prophecy is a prophecy of God's promised restoration of Israel, and it will occur in the near future.

The word "Israel" has two meanings. It refers to the entire house of Israel and northern Israel. Even now, people do not use the word "Israel" in these two senses. At present, Israel is the Jewish Republic. This is a one-sided name that strays far from the true meaning of the Bible, which is Israel's creator.

The prophet Isaiah in the Bible said:

"He will gather together the dispersed of Israel, And assemble the dispersed of Judah from the four corners of the earth. The jealousy of Ephraim will be departed, And the enemies of Judah will be cut off. Ephraim will not be jealous of Judah, nor will Judah be his adversary." (Isaiah 11:12, 13)
In this way, the restoration of Israel is prophesied separately, with a comprehensive restoration of the north and a comprehensive restoration of the south.

Prophets often refer to all of Israel as Israel, with southern Israel represented by Judah and northern Israel represented by Ephraim. Isaiah is not alone in this. The prophet Ezekiel also states:
"For all the house of Israel will serve me; there I will accept them with open arms; there I will require your offerings and your best offerings along with all your holy things" (Ezekiel 20:40).

Ezekiel further prophesied that Israel would be gathered from the nations where they had been scattered. Furthermore, in chapter 36, he teaches us about Israel's humiliation:

"Prophesy over the land of Israel, saying, 'I will speak of my jealousy in my wrath, because you have been reproached by the nations.'"

Ezekiel chapter 37 clarifies whether the name Israel refers simply to the entire house, or to southern Israel, representing Judah, or whether northern Israel is not included. It is not appropriate to confuse these two terms. Ezekiel promises, "Branch, you mountains of Israel, and bear fruit for my people Israel, for their return is near."

In the next chapter, chapter 37, Ezekiel speaks of the prophecy of the dry bones crouching in the famous valley:

"These bones are the whole house of Israel... Son of man, take one staff and write on it, 'For Judah, and for the children of Israel with him.' Take another staff and write on it, 'For the staff of Ephraim, for Joseph, and for all the house of Israel with him.' Join them together as one staff; they shall be one in your hand."

In this way, Israel is referred to as the branch of Judah and Ephraim, and prophecies were made for each of them. The Jews returned to their own nation, the land of Palestine, which they once called Canaan, and restored their country in the mid-20th century. And they, Judah (the Jews), are searching for the people whom the Bible calls Israel, led by their brother Ephraim, along with the other nine tribes, and many Jews from southern Israel, also known as Eastern Judea. You can probably already guess where in the world there is a nation of peoples who live in such a place, land. In that place, or rather in that nation, a worldwide faith in God will be resurrected.

I will end my talk here. Thank you very much.

Lost Tribes Institute

Japan and Bible Forum

Sons of Joseph

will grow into a multitude upon the earth

by

Margot Crossing

Founder: Lost Tribes Institute

Exploring the promises to nations, like Japan, through the themes of fish and multiplying like fish, fishermen and their catches

Introduction

In this paper, presented in Tokyo, in collaboration with our Japanese colleagues at the Japan and Bible Forum, I would like to take a few themes, which align with my main premise, as stated in the paper "Restoration of Israel"[1], that are in accordance with Japanese culture. As in the story of the "two brothers" that has a Kyrgyz parallel – there once were two brothers, one ate fish and he became the Japanese, and the other ate meat, and we don't know where he is.[2]

The Japanese are a fishing culture so I will use the themes of fish, fishermen, sand, and seashore as motifs to relay this message.

Today, Israel and especially God's purposes for Israel, may invoke various emotions and even contentious and differing world views. I would like to take the promises to Jacob's son Joseph and his two boys in regards to them 'multiplying upon the face of the earth' as a subset and show how they apply to Japan and nations like them. Israel in our context here refers to the House of Israel – aka the House of Ephraim, the Ten Tribes.

Pattern and design for Israel and all nations

I will look at the pattern or design for Israel and mankind, through some Old Testament prophecies and show how they fit perfectly into New Testament prophecies and types and shadows.

Prophecy

- To Joseph and his sons - Genesis 48:16

The Angel which redeemed me from all evil, bless the lads; and let my name be named on them, and the name of my fathers Abraham and Isaac; and let them grow [dagah] *into a multitude in the midst of the earth.*

- Judah - Genesis 49:10

The sceptre shall not depart from Judah, nor a lawgiver from between his feet, until Shiloh comes; and unto him shall the gathering of the people be.

Here, there is the continuation of the prophecies to Abraham that his descendants would be as the stars in the heavens and the sand on the seashore – unable to be counted for sheer numbers. Joseph and his two boys, Ephraim and Manasseh, are included in the multiplication and blessings prophecies. The word "grow" in verse 16 comes from the Hebrew 'dagah', which has the same root as fish and implies that they would spawn and swarm as fish in the sea of the nations. Judah and the other brothers have various blessings given before Jacob's death. To Judah would be the scepter and lawgiver until Shiloh comes. This is recognised by both Jews and Christians as a reference to the Messiah. Christians, of course, see Yeshua as that person.

Jews await the Messiah for the in-gathering of the twelve tribes of Israel. One of our aims at Lost Tribes Institute is to demonstrate that Yeshua has already fulfilled the expectation of gathering the twelve tribes of Israel. He has done that by sending His apostles to the very places that the Israelites had settled. This paper will show, although briefly, that Yeshua has been finding and gathering the twelve tribes scattered in the nations through the fishermen disciples that He raised up. This was true in the first five centuries and this pattern has repeated itself in the last two centuries.

The blueprint

The God of Creation, who made man and woman to be fruitful, multiply, and look after the earth, made a covenant with Abram that he would become the father of many nations – Abraham[3]. This was reiterated to Isaac, Jacob and then to Joseph's sons.

- Prophecy of Jacob's blessing to Ephraim and Manasseh

Genesis 48:19

Gen 48:19 And his father refused, and said, I know it, my son, I know it: he also shall become a people, and he also shall be great: but truly his younger brother shall be greater than he, and his seed shall become a ***multitude*** *of nations.* KJV

By splitting the nation of Israel into two after King Solomon, God was able to simultaneously cause one part to multiply into nations, whilst making the other part to continually have a King on David's throne until Shiloh came. Shiloh or the Messiah would open ***the way to God*** to all those in the multitude of nations that Joseph's boys would become.

How was ***the way to God*** open? It was by the God of Heaven sending the Son of God to fulfil all the righteous traditions and then allowing the Spirit of the God of Creation to dwell in the hearts of man and cause man to know inwardly what laws and traditions he needed to do to please God and also what not to.

We know this as the New Covenant, and it is made only with the House of Israel and the House of Judah. This implies that when Abraham and ultimately Ephraim's seed is distributed throughout all nations that this should be understood that the House of Israel is synonymous with the nations.[4]

The prophecy to Ephraim is the meaning of Paul's all Israel

*Genesis 48:19 But his father refused and said, "I know, my son, I know; he also will become a people, and he also will be great. However, his younger brother shall be greater than he, and his seed shall become the **fullness** of nations."* LSB

The Legacy Standard Bible interchanges *multitude* and *fullness* in verse nineteen; and "*nations*" has the same meaning in the Greek and the Hebrew, "*ethnos*" and "Goyim", which is translated as "gentiles", and so this connects Genesis 48:19 to Romans 11:25-27 through the phrase "fullness of the gentiles"/ "multitude of nations".

As with the "until" in verse 49:10 above, Romans chapter eleven has an "until" followed by a "so". This implies a causative relation between the "Fullness of the Gentiles" and "all Israel being saved".[5] Ephraim's seed is to be 'alloyed' with the nations and then restored back to the Kingdom of Israel through Messiah, king of Judah, so it is in this way that ALL ISRAEL WILL BE SAVED.

Romans 11:25-27 For I do not want you, brothers, to be uninformed of this mystery—so that you will not be wise in your own estimation—that a partial hardening has happened to Israel *until* the fullness of the Gentiles has come in; **26** *and so* all Israel will be saved; just as it is written,

"THE DELIVERER WILL COME FROM ZION,
HE WILL REMOVE UNGODLINESS FROM JACOB."
27 "AND THIS IS [c]MY COVENANT WITH THEM,
WHEN I TAKE AWAY THEIR SINS."

Japan - implications

So what does that imply for Japan? It implies that, like many other nations, they are full of Ephraim's[6] seed. There is a partial blindness until the time of the fullness of the Gentiles (nations). Nations are restored back into covenant with the 'August' God of Creation. It is through the New Covenant that was promised to both the House of Judah and the House of Israel, by the deliverer [or may we say "Shiloh"] coming from Zion and taking away Jacob's sins.

Who is that deliverer? Why, the one who called young fishermen to follow Him and after His completion of removing sin[7] He called those young men to go to the ends of the earth – the isles and coastlines far off – and fish for men.

This New Covenant

This New Covenant also removes any structured religious intermediary or authority. For the understanding is in our hearts and knowing will be within each one of us on how we are to be sons of the Living God. It will be a direct father (Creator God) and son relationship. It will happen through the doorway or gate of Messiah (Son of the God) and the infilling of the Spirit of the God of Creation.

Lost Tribes Found

We have until now looked at the theology and prophecies regarding God's place for mankind through Abraham and his descendants. Let us look at where the so-called "Lost Tribes" went. And then we will ask if any, some or all have/had been found?

Where did the tribes go before, during and after the 740-722BC?

Below is Steven M Collins' map showing the dispersion of the Ten Tribes both East and West.

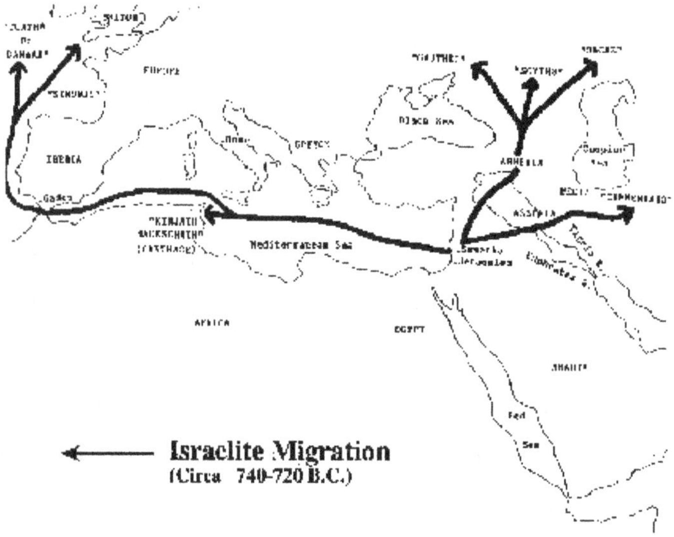

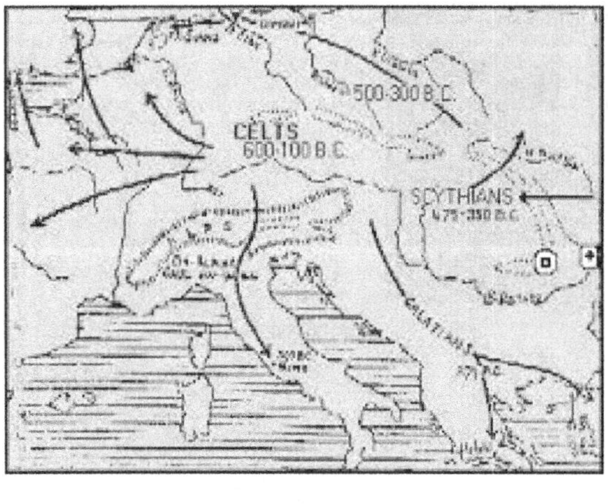

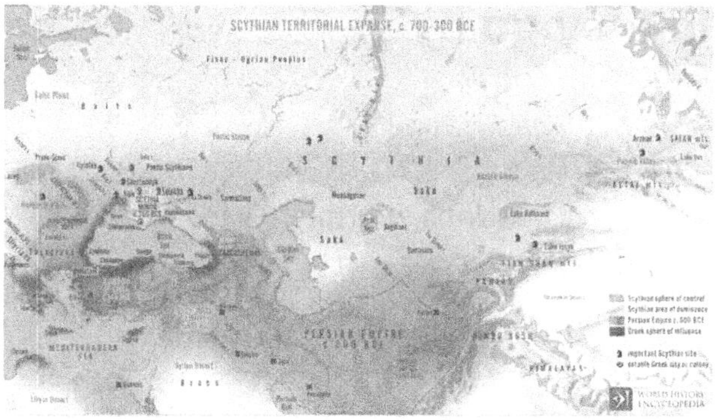

A map illustrating the expansion of the warrior nomad Scythians between the 7th and 3rd century BCE across Asia and Europe.

Scythians went both east and west and are recognised within the academic Lost Tribe researchers as Israelites. They are then recognised as Saka in the east and Sacae or Saxons in the west. The orange shading in the above right hand map shows the distribution of the Saka Empire between the 7th and 3rd centuries BCE.

The map below is 600 BCE and it shows the Iranian speaking peoples in green. They include the Tocharian Peoples, Saka, Massagatae, Parthians and Sogdians. The northern kingdom had been taken captive by Assyria and placed on their northern border to protect Assyria's territory from invasion from the north. No doubt they were speaking an Iranian dialect when they moved out from Assyrian and Persian spheres of influence.

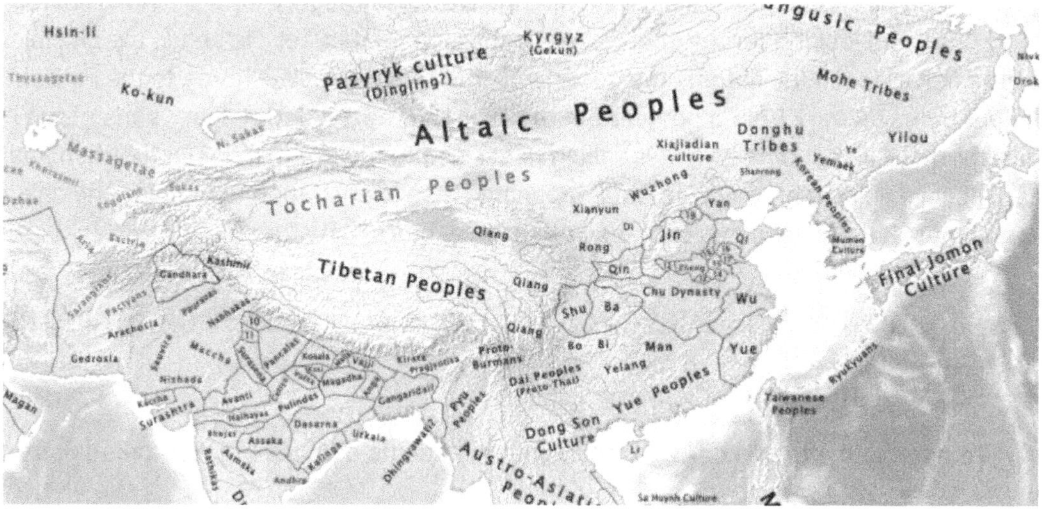

What names did they go by?

In the east …..

What names did they go by? In the east …..•Saka, •Scyths, •Parthia, •Qiang, •Hata, •Yuezhis, •Kyrgyz

What names did they go by? In the west….•Khumri, Cymri, Celts•Scyths, •Cimmerian, •Saxon, Sacae, Alans, Goths, Visy Goths

Below are two maps showing the migration of the Ten Tribes into Europe and the British Isles.

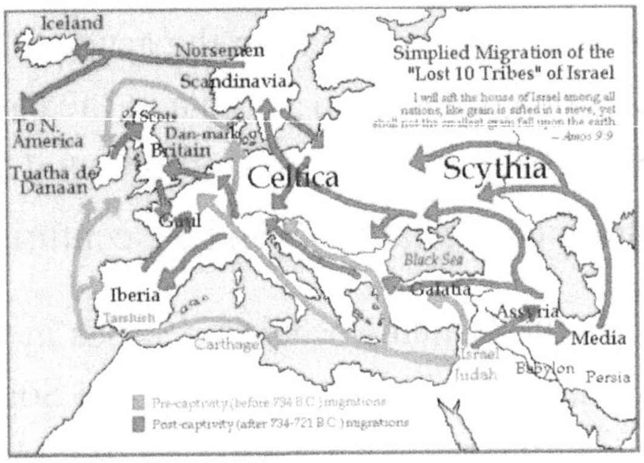

Dispersed Israel restored to the Kingdom

The Jews are expecting that Messiah will be the instrument of restoration of the northern kingdom. Another of his names is Shiloh. Those people of ―the way‖,useimagery from Yeshua Himself,thatHe is the Good Shepherd looking for the Lost Sheep of the House of Israel. He sends his disciples to the ―ends of the earth‖ to tell the nations the goodnews that they can come home to the Father. They will no longer be ―Lo Ammi ―not a people‖ but they will now be ―B'ney el chai ―sons of the living God‖. Another motif is that of the Master calling fishermen to fish for men instead of fish.It is this motif that I believe holds a prophecy to both Japan and also every nation containing the children of Israel. Let us look at the miraculous catches of fish in Yeshua's ministry.

Miracles of huge hauls of fish –beginning and end of Yeshua's ministry on earth

In the New Testament the themes of fishermen and miraculous catches bracket the ministry of Yeshua.

Fishermen called to follow–the beginning

Matthew 4:18 Now as Jesus was walking by the Sea of Galilee, He saw two brothers, Simon who was called Peter, and Andrew his brother, casting a net into the sea; for they were fishermen. 19 And He said to them, "Follow Me, and I will make you fishers of men." 20 And immediately they left their nets and followed Him. 21 And going on from there He saw two other brothers, James the son of Zebedee, and John his brother, in the boat with Zebedee their father, mending their nets; and He called them. 22 And immediately they left the boat and their father, and followed Him.

Why did they follow Jesus?

Luke 5:1 Once while Jesus was standing beside the lake of Gennesaret(Galilee) and the crowd was pressing in on him to hear the word of God, 2 he saw two boats there at the shore of the lake; the fishermen had gone out of them and were washing their nets. 3 He got into one of the boats, the one belonging to Simon, and asked him to put out a little way from the shore. Then he sat down and taught the crowds from the boat. 4 When he had finished speaking, he said to Simon, "Put out into the deep water and let down your nets for a catch." 5 Simon answered, "Master, we have worked all night long but have caught nothing. Yet if you say so, I will let down the nets." 6 When they had done this, they caught so many fish that their nets were beginning to break. 7 So they signaled their partners in the other boat to come and help them. And they came and filled both boats, so that they began to sink. 8 But when Simon Peter saw it, he fell down at Jesus' knees, saying, "Go away from me, Lord, for I am a sinful man!" 9 For he and all who were with him were amazed at the catch of fish that they had taken; 10 and so also were James and John, sons of Zebedee, who were partners with Simon. Then Jesus said to Simon, "Do not be afraid; from now on you will be catching people." 11 When they had brought their boats to shore, they left everything and followed him.LSB

Lost Tribes Found by apostolic fishermen & their progeny -beginning

It is an historic fact that the people of 'The Way', the followers of Messiah, multiplied disciples among the Judeans and then went to and found the Israelites in Asia Minor, Black Sea regions, the coasts of the Mediterranean and the British Isles. Much has been written on this including our own Mikkel Kragh.[9]

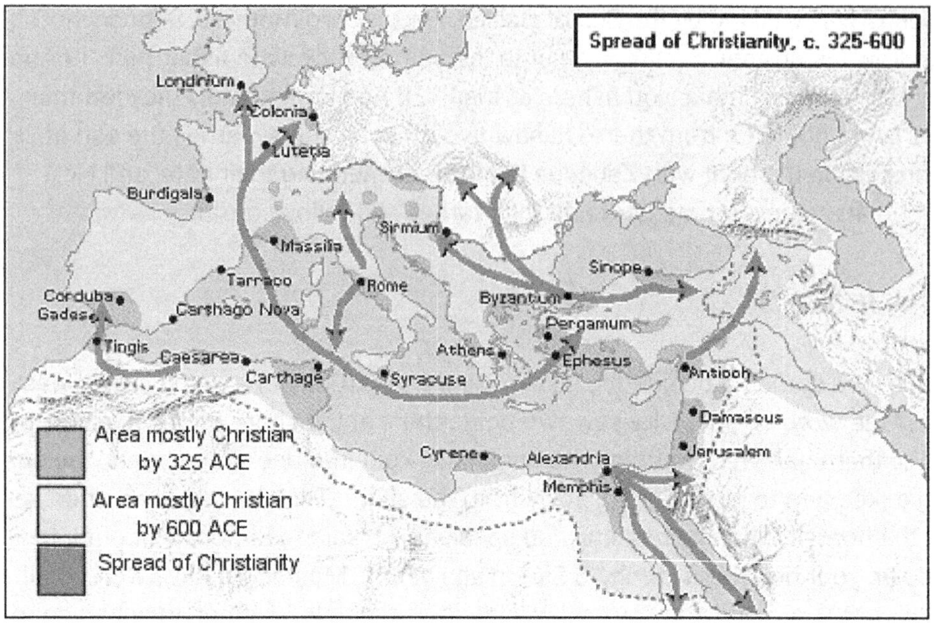

Thomas went to the east and found Israelites along the coasts of India.[10] He even travelled to China[11] with God's message. See my Restoration paper[12] for more detail. Christianity did indeed follow the pathways of the Ten Tribes, for they had an expectation and were waiting for the Messiah. It was Yeshua's stated objective and prophetic mandate to gather in the tribes to Himself.

Fishermen called to the larger mission

John 21:1 After these things Jesus manifested Himself again to the disciples at the Sea of Tiberias, and He manifested Himself in this way. 2 Simon Peter, and Thomas called Didymus, and Nathanael of Cana in Galilee, and the sons of Zebedee, and two others of His disciples were together. 3 Simon Peter said to them, "I am going fishing." They said to him, "We will also come with you." They went out and got into the boat; and that night they caught nothing.4 But when the day was now breaking, Jesus stood on the beach;yet the disciples did not know that it was Jesus. 5 So Jesus said to them, "Children, do you have any fish?" They answered Him, "No." 6 And He said to them, "Cast the net on the right side of the boat and you will find some." So they cast, and then they were not able to haul it in because of the great number of fish. 7 Therefore that disciple whom Jesus loved said to Peter, "It is the Lord." So when Simon Peter heard that it was the Lord, he put his outer garment on (for he was stripped for work), and cast himself into the sea. 8 But the other disciples came in the little boat, for they were not far from the land, but about two hundred cubits away, dragging the net full of fish.9 So when they got out on the land, they saw a charcoal fire in place and fish placed on it, and bread. 10 Jesus said to them, "Bring some of the fish which you have now caught." 11 Simon Peter went up and drew the net to land, full of large fish, 153; and although there were so many, the net was not torn.

Prophetically, this closing miracle speaks of the end of this age

The miraculous catch at the closing of Yeshua's ministry on earth, I believe, foreshadows a greater harvest of souls (fish) at the close of this age[13]. We have great examples of the pattern of Israelites or ―Lost Tribes‖ coming back to the Father, the great creator, in astonishing numbers among the Karen around 1830 and the Mizo about 1920. Both these groups are represented at our symposium.Our other representative from Kyrgyzstan,Nasira, and Dr PC Biaksiama, a Mizo,have what appears to be a relic of tradition and a linguistic nomenclature that points directly to Joseph. Nasira's grandmother, in the rural area of Kyrgyzstan, would pray with Nasira to the God of Abraham, Jakyb and Josef. Lienboi, from our first symposium in Aizawl, Mizoram, postulated that Zo from Mizo or Zomi is a phonic shift from Yo as in Yosef. ‗Mi' means people, so the people of Zo or Yo. The Mizo also are famous for passing down the name of Manasi or Manmasi, which is an unmistakable reference to Manasseh -so too, the Kyrgyz'hero,Manas. ConclusionMaybe the closing of this age will also be brought about by apostolic fishermen seeking the Lost Tribes. The examples of the Karen and the Mizo are a down payment, or first-fruits of something far greater. That will include an awakening and a remembering among the Japanese and the Kyrgyz. Also the rekindling of a fire in China's southwest and then again in greater India.If Europe and the Saxon Celtic peoples revisit their shared histories then indeed a very great regathering would take place. It is very interesting that the one hundred and fifty-three fish did not cause the disciples'nets to break.

MY PRAYER. ABBA FATHER, CAUSE OUR JAPANESE COLLEAGUES TO CONTINUALLY CAST THEIR NETS AND MAY THEIR NETS NEVER BREAK.

Bibliography

Allen, J.H., Judah's Scepter and Joseph's Birthright, Originally published, 1902. Nineteenth Edition. Re-typeset, A.D. 20002.

Avichail, R. Eliyahu., The Tribes of Israel 5765 Amishav Jerusalem
Barker, Margaret,. Temple Theology –An Introduction23rdApril 2004 SPCK Publishing
Capt, E Raymond, Missing Links Discovered in Assyrian Tablets, 19855.
Chen, Esther., The Hidden Q'iang –Sons of SheepAbridged edition English
Chung, Ha-Sang Howard Dispersion of the Israelites in the Eurasian Continent: How GOD has fulfilled His Promise: History of Eurasia from Biblical Perspective Amazon Paperback –July 27, 20237.
Collins, Steven M., Israel's Lost Empires2004 Bible Blessings Royal Oak M.I.
Collins, Steven M., ParthiaThe forgotten Ancient Superpower and its role in Biblical History2004 Bible Blessings Royal Oak M.I.
Drummond Joseph F, 2300 Days of Hell2014 Xlibris Corporation,
Gawler, Col.J.C., Our Scythian Ancestors Identified with Israel
Grant, Asahel; The Nestorians or the Lost TribesJohn Murray, London 184112.Heim, Arnold Minya Gongkar 1933 Verlag Hans Huber, Bern-Berlin
Halkin, Hillel. Across the Sabbath River2002 Houghton Mi→in Company New York
Lendering, Jona Alexander the Great The Demise of the Persian Empire,[340-320BC] 2004 Athenaeum Polak & Van Gennep Amsterdam
Lenthang, Dr Khuplam Milui. The Wonderful Tales of the Manmasi (Kuki-Chin-Mizo) 2013 Maxford Books Delhi.
Mallory, J.P. & Mair, Victor H. The Tarim Mummies: Ancient China and the Mystery of the Earliest Peoples from the WestThames & Hudson, 2000 -Social Science –352 pages
Moore, George M.D. The Lost Tribes and the Saxons of the East and of the West: With new views of Buddhism, and translations of rock-records in India1861 London, Longmans, Green, Longman, and Roberts
Moore, Thomas History of Ireland1843 Lea & Blanchard, Philadelphia
Rafy, Mrs. Folk-tales of the Kharsi, MacMillian & Co London 192020.Rice, Tamara Talbot, The Scythians3rd edition 1961 F.A. Praeger
Richardson, Don Eternity in their hearts3rd Ed. 2005 Regal Books. Ventura, California
Risbek (Hewitt, Richard) Manas -Lost & Found: A Bridge Linking Kyrgyzstan's Epic toAncient Oracles2012 Risbek California
Richard Hewitt et al. The Interconnectedness of the Israelites in Asia: Lost Tribes Institute's First Scientific Symposium by Richard Hewitt (Author), Margot Crossing (Author), Arimasa Kubo (Author), Kengo Nagami (Author), & 6 more Published on Amazon Dec 2023
Rongphar, Sonaram. Head of the United Mikir's Research Society. Various papers given to this author.
Shachan, Dr Avigdor, In the Footsteps of the Ten Lost Tribes2007 CreateSpace Translated from the Hebrew 2003 version Towards the Sambatyon River -a Journey in the Footsteps of the Ten TribesHakibbutz Hameuchad Pub. House,Tel Aviv
Shu-min Huang & Cheng-kuang Hsu Imaging China: Regional Division and National Unity Ed.Taipei: Institute of Ethnology. http://ultra.ihp.sinica.edu.tw/~origins/pages/barbarbook4.htm Accessed 15/4/1627.
Spykermann, Stephen J. A Game changing revelation:The Hidden Ancestry of America & Great Britain September 2014 Legends Library Publishing NY
Torrance, Rev. Thomas T., China's First Missionaries: Ancient 'Israelites '2nd Edition 1988 Daniel Shaw Co. Chicago.
Zaithanchhungi, Israel-Mizo Identity2008 Hope Lodge, AizawlQR code to Restoration of Israel leads to the Restoration of all things

---

Contact Margot Crossing
Blog https://losttribesfoundblog.wordpress.com/
Rumbel https://rumble.com/user/LostTribesFoundAcademia
https://losttribesinstitute.academia.edu/MargotCROSSING

A Brief Comparison of Southeast Asia's Karen People with Ancient Israel

By Anchalee Khamsirisuk Boschmann

The Karen people are one of the oldest ethnic groups in Southeast Asia. Spread primarily across the hills of eastern Myanmar and northwestern Thailand, they are known for their musicality, vibrant cultural traditions, and strong sense of communal identity. The Karen are also known for their beliefs, which appear enigmatic for a people surrounded by Animist and Buddhist cultures. The Karen's history is not fully understood, but clues found in their beliefs, traditions, and the memory of a "Lost Book" suggest a connection to ancient Israel and other "Lost Book" peoples across Asia.

Although it may seem unlikely from a geographical perspective, the suggestion that the Karen people are a lost branch of Israel has considerable merit. Furthermore, the Karen may be a key element to uncovering the eastern dispersion of the exiled tribes that were once the nation of Israel. This is due to the Karen people's absolute dedication to maintaining their cultural roots through oral tradition and ceremony. For nearly three thousand years, in what can only be described as a miraculous accomplishment, the Karen have successfully preserved the essence of their ancestors.

Consider this: These migrant exiles wandered across unfamiliar lands, living only from what the earth provided, without a written language and often without rights in the countries they crossed. The Karen story reveals their extraordinary resilience and quiet achievement.

Although there are many cultural aspects to investigate, the best evidence of their origin can be found in the poems and oral traditions. From the content of their poems (known as tha in the Karen Sgaw language), it becomes apparent that the Karen are indeed a remnant of a great nation. A nation with total conviction that their laws and values were given to them by God, the creator. In the same manner that the ancient Israelites believed.

Who are the Karen

It was not until the 1800s that the Karen people became known to the Western world. Fortunately, missionaries, such as Francis Mason, had the foresight to document the culture. In the early 1800s, the Karen were still mostly unaffected by Buddhism and totally unaware of Christianity. Nearly all the Karen of that era were animists with a particular set of beliefs that seemed to fit better in the Middle East than the jungles of Southeast Asia.

Today, Karen culture includes Christians, Buddhists, and Animists, and there is often overlap between the groups. This mixing of customs has complicated research into the origin of the Karen. However, the missionaries of the 1800s observed the Karen in their most pure state. It is from their observations that we can learn the most.

The term "Karen" refers to a diverse group of about 7 million people. The major subgroups include the Karen Sgaw and the Karen Pwo. They each have their own language and cultural traditions. Before the arrival of the British Empire, the various Karen tribes had their own independent territory along the Salween, Irrawaddy, and Tenasserim rivers in Eastern Burma and Northwestern Siam. The Karen consider themselves to be the original inhabitants of the region. During the colonial era, the British employed Karen people in administrative and military roles, partly due to their adopted Christian faith and Westernized sensibilities. When the British left the region, the Karen nations were lumped into the country of Burma, along with many other tribes and nations that comprise modern Myanmar. The resulting clash of cultures and the cruel oppression of the Bamar majority erupted into a civil war, ongoing since 1949.

Generations of war have made life very difficult for the Karen tribes. Many have crossed the Salween River and now live in refugee camps at the Thai border. Karen villages are bombed and burned regularly. This has been devastating for the culture, causing many important historical details to be lost.

The Karen on the Thai side of the border have a much better life, but modernization has caused them to lose touch with many of their traditions. This makes research more difficult, but there are still some who remember the stories and are happy to share.

The Karen is the official name of this people group, but it is not the name they use exclusively. The name Karen is probably an adaptation of Kayin, or Kariang by the British. These are the Bamar and Mon/Tai words for the Karen. A more appropriate name is Pgaz K' Nyau (sounds like Pa'ginyo), which the British must have found difficult to pronounce. Today, the word Karen is used officially, while Pgaz K' Nyau is used among the people.

The two main Karen languages belong to the Sino-Tibetan family, which missionaries adapted to the Burmese script in the 19th century.

Evidence of the Israel/Karen Connection

As this is intended to be only a brief introduction to the topic, I will follow the example of Francis Mason and present only some of the best evidence, most of which he compiled for his articles to the Calcutta Christian Observer in 1834.

Through his personal observations of the Karen, Mason was fully convinced that the Karen were indeed a branch of ancient Israel. I will summarize some of the evidence he used to arrive at this conclusion.

The best record we have of Karen beliefs and traditions comes from their poems or *thas*, as they are called by the Karen. As you will see, the poems often employ repetition and parallel phrasing, a technique also commonly found in Hebrew poetry. Karen poems often repeat lines with minor changes to drive home meaning. Another similarity between the poems and Hebrew poetry is that they both serve a didactic purpose: preserving tradition, laws, prophecy, and ethics.

The Karen Worship an Eternal Creator God

God is unchangeable, eternal,

He was in the beginning of the world;

God is endless, eternal,

He existed in the beginning of the world:

God is truly unchangeable and eternal,

He existed in ancient time at the beginning of the world.

The life of God is endless.

The Name of the Karen Creator God is Y'wa

The resemblance between the Karen word Y'wa, and the Hebrew word Jehovah is unmistakable. The Christian Karen do not doubt that Y'wa is the same Jehovah. It is not even debated. Furthermore, there is in some of the poems, a warning not to call God Y'wa. The same paradox is found in the Hebrew traditions. Today, many Jews will not utter the name Jehovah or write it in full.

O my children and grandchildren! Call not God Y'wa;

by calling him Y'wa, he will never return to us.

Karen Songs (Thas) Contain Critical Components of the Hebrew Old Testament

The Creation of Man and Woman

God created us in ancient times,

And has a perfect knowledge of all things.

Call him not Y'wa, but call him great ancestor:

When people call his name, he hears.

Woman Was Formed from the Rib of Man

O children and grandchildren!

Woman at first was a rib of man,

therefore, woman ought to obey man in all things.

Fall of Man

Temptation, temptation, the fruit of temptation.

The fruit of temptation dropped ripe:

The fruit of temptation was bad.

It poisoned to death our mother.

The fruit of temptation, ' Do thou eat it not.'

In the beginning, it poisoned our mother and father to death.

The tree of death came by woman.

The tree of life by man.

Tower of Babel

Men were all brethren.

They had all the language of God,

But they disbelieved the language of God,

And became enemies to each other.

Because they disbelieved God,

Their language is divided.

God gave them commands,

But they did not believe him,

and divisions ensued.

The Karen Have a Collection of Moral Laws Similar to the Ten Commandments

Here are a few examples of the Karen moral laws.

Love God

O children and grandchildren! love God, and never so much as mention his name,

for by speaking his name, he goes farther and farther from us.

No Idols

O children and grandchildren! do not worship idols or priests.

If you worship them, you derive no advantage thereby

while you increase your sins exceedingly.

Honor Your Parents

O children and grandchildren! Respect and reverence your mother and father,

for when you were small, they did not suffer so much as a mosquito to bite you.

To sin against your parents is a heinous crime.

Love Others

O children and grandchildren! Live in peace with each other.

God from heaven observes us, and we are manifest to him.

If we do not love each other, God will not love us:

but if we love one another, God will look down upon you with joy.

Do Not Murder

O children and grandchildren! Do not take the life of a man.

If you kill, you must bear your sin. In the next world, you will be killed in return.

Do Not Steal

O children and grandchildren! Do not steal the goods of another,

for the owner worked for them until he sweated. Thieves will have to repay.

Do Not Commit Adultery

O children and grandchildren!

Do not commit adultery or fornication with the child or wife of another,

female or male;

for the righteous one looks down from above,

and these things are exposed to him.

Those who do thus will go to hell.

Do Not Lie

O children and grandchildren! Do not speak falsehood.

What you do not know, do not speak.

Liars shall have their tongues cut out.

O children and grandchildren! Do not use deceitful language,

but speak the words of truth only.

The righteous one in heaven knows everything that is said.

Do Not Covet

O children and grandchildren!

Do not covet the things of others, nor desire to accumulate property,

But work according to your ability and covet not.

The Karen Believe They Are Wanderers Cast Out by God

Another interesting parallel with Israel is the fact that they believe they were cast out of their land by God. The Hebrew scriptures contain prophetic warnings that Israel would be sent into exile. The Israelites believe their fall and exile were ordered by God because of their unfaithfulness or adultery before God. The word adultery is used several times in the Hebrew scriptures to describe the worship of foreign gods. The word adultery is also used by the Karen to describe unfaithfulness to God.

The dead rose again when the plantain leaf was yellow.

But Satan produced sin;

The dead rose to life when the plantain leaf was yellow.

But Satan introduced sin;

Thou hast committed adultery against God;

hence in this state thou hast no honor.

The Karen Believe They Will Be Restored by God to God

O children and grandchildren! Formerly, God loved the Karen nation above all others, but they transgressed his commands, and in consequence of their transgressions, we suffer as at present. Because God cursed us, we are in our present afflicted state and have no books. But God will again have mercy on us, and again he will love us above all others. God will yet save us again; it is on account of our listening to the language of Satan that we thus suffer.

The Hebrew scriptures echo the restoration of the lost tribes to God.

Isaiah 11:11–12 – On that day the Lord will reach out his hand a second time to reclaim the surviving remnant of his people... He will raise a banner for the nations and gather the exiles of Israel.

Jeremiah 23:3 – I myself will gather the remnant of my flock out of all the countries where I have driven them and will bring them back to their pasture.

Jeremiah 31:10 – He who scattered Israel will gather them and will watch over his flock like a shepherd.

The Karen Calendar

Interestingly, the Karen maintain their own calendar, which begins in the year 739 BC of the Gregorian calendar. At this time, Tiglath-Pileser III of Assyria had just begun his expansion into Israel with the capture of the strategic city of Arpad. This is the battle that set the stage for the eventual collapse and capture of Israel in 722 BC.

The Assyrian Empire, under the reign of King Tiglath-Pileser III, began its incursions into the northern kingdom around 740 BC. The final blow came during the reign of King Hoshea, the last king of Israel. In 722 BC, the Assyrian king Shalmaneser V laid siege to Samaria, the capital of the northern kingdom. The siege lasted for three years, culminating in the capture of the city by Sargon II, Shalmaneser's successor. The biblical account in 2 Kings 17:6 states: In the ninth year of Hoshea, the king of Assyria captured Samaria and deported the

Israelites to Assyria. He settled them in Halah, in Gozan on the Habor River, and in the cities of the Medes.

The Karen Did Not Worship Idols

The prophet Hosea said Israel would have no idols:

For the children of Israel shall abide many days without a king, and without a prince, and without a sacrifice, and without an image, and without an ephod, and without teraphim: Hosea 3:4

The Karen Expect a Restoration to a Great City

> Good persons, the good, Shall go to the silver town, the silver city;
>
> Righteous persons, the righteous, Shall go to the new town, the new city;
>
> Persons that believe their father and mother, Shall enjoy the golden palace.

This is a parallel to the Hebrew tradition of a new heaven and a new Jerusalem made of gold and precious stones.

> O thou afflicted, tossed with tempest, and not comforted,
>
> behold, I will lay thy stones with fair colours,
>
> and lay thy foundations with sapphires.
>
> And I will make thy windows of agates,
>
> and thy gates of carbuncles,
>
> and all thy borders of pleasant stones. Isaiah 54:11-12

The Karen Believe in a Coming King

This king will be king of all the earth, ushering in an era of peace and the end of poverty:

When the Karen king arrives,
There will be only one monarch;
When the Karen king comes,
There will be neither rich nor poor;
When the Karen king shall come,
Rich and poor will not exist.
When the Karen king arrives,
Everything will be happy;
When the Karen king arrives,
The beasts will be happy;
When Karens have a king,
Lions and leopards will lose their savageness.

Isaiah 11:1-7 is an amazing parallel to this poem:

And there shall come forth a rod out of the stem of Jesse,
and a Branch shall grow out of his roots:
And the spirit of the LORD shall rest upon him,
the spirit of wisdom and understanding,
the spirit of counsel and might,
the spirit of knowledge and of the fear of the LORD;
And shall make him of quick understanding in the fear of the LORD:
and he shall not judge after the sight of his eyes,
neither reprove after the hearing of his ears:
But with righteousness shall he judge the poor,
and reprove with equity for the meek of the earth:

and he shall smite the earth with the rod of his mouth,

and with the breath of his lips shall he slay the wicked.

And righteousness shall be the girdle of his loins,

and faithfulness the girdle of his reins.

The wolf also shall dwell with the lamb,

and the leopard shall lie down with the kid;

and the calf and the young lion and the fatling together;

and a little child shall lead them.

And the cow and the bear shall feed;

their young ones shall lie down together:

and the lion shall eat straw like the ox.

There is also this from Psalms 72:8-11:

He shall have dominion also from sea to sea,

and from the River to the ends of the earth.

Those who dwell in the wilderness will bow before Him,

and His enemies will lick the dust.

The kings of Tarshish and of the isles shall bring presents;

the kings of Sheba and Seba shall offer gifts.

Yes, all kings shall fall down before Him;

all nations shall serve Him.

Only the first seven verses of Isaiah are shown above, but the subject of the entire chapter is the coming king - the Messiah. Incredibly, there are a total of four Karen poems that intersect and mirror the subject matter of Isaiah 11, a chapter devoted to the lost tribes of Israel.

The Similarities Between the Karen and Israel Are Only in Aspects of the First Temple Era

When it was first realized that the Karen poems coincided with scripture, much debate was made about where the Karen would have learned these stories. The first suspicion was that early Christian missionaries could have introduced the Bible to the Karen. But there was no content in the oral tradition that included the story of Jesus, the primary focus of Christian teachings. The alternative was that these stories came from the Jews, but that didn't explain why the Karen poems only included details known by Israelites up to the First Temple era.

Since some of these traditions are so definite and truthful, they must have been derived directly from the Bible, and as they contain nothing peculiarly Christian, they could not have come from persons acquainted with the New Testament. They are all Old Testament traditions...

Some Core Traditions of the Animist Karen

Despite maintaining their cultural essence for thousands of years, it has been harder for the Karen to do so in the last two centuries. The influence of Buddhism, Christianity, westernization, and seven decades of war and oppression has made change inevitable. Therefore, it is the traditions of the Animist Karen that offer the most valuable insight into the tribes' way of life before the introduction of Buddhism and Christianity.

Care of the Land

The Animist Karen are people of the land; harmony with the land is integral to their way of life. They believe that rivers, forests, and mountains are inhabited by K'thi or spirits. They maintain sacred groves of trees. For example, some trees are dedicated after the birth of a child, and that tree can never be cut down. The grove becomes a registry of births. Cutting a sacred tree will offend the spirits and result in sickness.

When the Karen wish to use an area of a forest, they must make a spirit house and ask the creator God, Y'wa K'jah, permission. Before a field is cleared, a sacrifice must be made, and the blood is offered to spirits for a blessing on the field. Boundary rocks and posts, marked with blood, may also be used for protection.

The Karen Practice Rotational Farming

Although they practice a slash-and-burn style of agriculture, they do so in a sustainable manner. Many mature trees are protected and left standing. Fields are farmed for only a couple of years, and then they are left alone to return to a natural state for seven to ten years.

Cultural Events

Every year, the Karen celebrate two essential cultural events: the Htav Meh Keh, or string ceremony, in August, and the Ta Yaw Ta Khau, or rice festival, which occurs at the new year.

Htav Meh Keh

The essential elements of life, water, fire, thread, and rice, are represented in the String ceremony called Htav Meh Keh. Rice is considered life, and it also represents God, the creator. In the ceremony, a cotton string is soaked in water, passed through a flame, and then pressed into rice. The string is then tied to someone's wrist. Everyone at the ceremony will receive a string on their wrist.

This community ceremony is centered on social and spiritual unity, but it also reinforces a bond to the land, ancestors, and the great ancestor (the creator god). By tying white strings on each other's wrists, villagers reaffirm harmony not only among themselves but also with their environment.

The string ceremony is a time for people to call their children back to their parents, to reinforce their beliefs, and to advise them against following other ways. The children are called with a trilling sound (Prrroo, prrroo), in the same manner they call their chickens. This is done so outsiders will not know what they are doing. This is a highly ceremonial occasion that features animal sacrifice to make amends for wrong actions (sins). For this ceremony, a small building is constructed to serve as an altar. Usually, a white fowl will be sacrificed, and its blood is spread on its posts. After the sacrifice, families go to their homes and stay there to eat and to spend the night. After the door is closed, no one is allowed to leave or enter until morning

A parallel can be drawn with Israel in this tradition. The Israelites considered blood to be life, and that blood must be used for atonement.

For the life of the flesh is in the blood: and I have given it to you upon the altar to make an atonement for your souls: for it is the blood that maketh an atonement for the soul. Leviticus 17:11

The Israelites sprinkled blood on the altar after a sacrifice for sin.

And Moses took half of the blood, and put it in basins; and half of the blood he sprinkled on the altar. And he took the book of the covenant, and read in the audience of the people: and they said, All that the LORD hath said will we do, and be obedient. And Moses took the blood, and sprinkled it on the people, and said, Behold the blood of the covenant, which the LORD hath made with you concerning all these words. Exodus 24:6-8

Karen rituals of marking posts or altars with animal blood for the protection of the household and crops are comparable to the Israelites' smearing blood on the doorposts during Passover. A ritual commemorating the first Passover, where blood on the doorposts protected the Israelites from the hand of God (the angel of death) during the 10th plague in Egypt.

And they shall take of the blood, and strike it on the two side posts and on the upper door post of the houses, wherein they shall eat it (the sacrificed lamb). Exodus 12:7

Ta Yaw Ta Khau, The Rice Festival

The Rice festival is usually held between November and January, depending on the lunar calendar. It often coincides with the New Year Celebrations.

At the Rice Festival, offerings of the first rice are made to the Creator God and to ancestral spirits to thank them for fertility and the harvest. Animal sacrifice (chicken, pig, or buffalo) may be part of the ritual to appease land spirits and ensure blessings for the next year. Rice wine is often prepared for communal drinking.

This is a time of community celebration. The village comes together to share a meal of rice, reinforcing their unity. Dancing, singing, and the playing of instruments: gongs (k'lee), buffalo horn trumpets, harps, and bamboo flutes are common.

Traditional songs praise the harvest, honor ancestors, and stories in the form of poems (Thas) recount their history and moral lessons.

In Karen culture, rice is seen as sacred, with its own "soul" (k'la). Offering the first portion is both a thanksgiving and an act of renewal.

A parallel with Israel can also be seen in this tradition. The Rice festival is reminiscent of the first fruits and the Harvest festivals of the Israelites. Leviticus 23.

As with the Israelites, the Animist Karen Have a List of Behaviors That Are Considered Taboo

1. Pregnancy and Birth

Birthplaces are taboo; the hut used for childbirth is sometimes burned or abandoned because spirits (k'la) are thought to linger there.

Parallels in Leviticus 12

2. Death and Spirits

Houses where someone dies may be abandoned, or a ritual cleansing must be performed.

Touching a corpse without ritual precautions can bring illness or bad luck.

Parallels in Numbers 19:11–16

3. Agriculture and Rice Taboos

First harvest rice cannot be eaten until the firstfruits offering is made to Y'wa or the spirits.

Parallels in Deuteronomy 26:1–3

4. Hunting and Killing Animals

After a hunt, rituals must be performed to cleanse the hunter and protect the village from the animal's spirit.

Parallels in Leviticus 17:13, Leviticus 11, and Deuteronomy 14:3

5. Marriage and Family

Marriage of a Karen with a person of another race was formerly strictly forbidden.

Cousin marriage is often taboo in traditional Karen culture.

Breaking clan exogamy rules (marrying within one's own hta or lineage group) is forbidden.

Parallels in Leviticus 18, Ezra 9:1-10, and Nehemiah 13:23-2

6. Menstruation

Women's menstrual blood is considered ritually impure; restrictions were placed on what women could touch during menstruation.

Parallels in Leviticus 15:19–24

7. Sacred Places

The small animist shrine or altar (hta ku or ku taw) built at the edge of villages must not be disturbed.

Blood sacrifices offered there consecrate the land; failure to observe the taboo of leaving it untouched may bring sickness or crop failure.

Parallels in Exodus 3:5, Leviticus 16:2, and Deuteronomy 12

Connections to Other Lost Book Peoples

The Karen are not the only ethnic group with stories of lost sacred books and distant monotheistic origins. Other examples include many Asian tribes. Some of these are the Lahu, Wa, Kachin, Mizo, Kuki, Chin, Karbi, Kyrgyz, Altai, and the Qiang in China.

What unites these groups is the presence of sacred memory—oral histories, symbols, and rituals that seem to align with biblical traditions. And especially the memory of a "Lost Book" that held the keys to life and happiness. Though the stories are different for every group, most versions agree that the book was given by God to his sons and that it contained rules for successful living. In all cases, the book is lost at some point, either eaten or burned, or both. The Altai believe their book was lost in a river crossing. Whatever the case, the loss of the book marked a loss of knowledge and a setback for the people. But there was a promise that some day a white brother would come and bring his own sacred book that would be the same as the book they had lost.

By the late 1820s, Adoniram Judson, the first American missionary to Burma, had experienced limited success in his evangelism among the Bamar people in Burma. It was not until a Karen man, Koh Tha Byu, who worked for him, realized the Bible Judson carried could be the sacred book of legend, and Judson the white brother. Koh Tha Byu became a devoted disciple and an evangelist to his people. A great many Karen also came to believe that the Christian Bible was their sacred lost book and converted to Christianity. Don Richardson describes this wonderfully in his book: Eternity in Their Hearts. He recounts the stories of people from several other tribes, including the Lahu, the Shan, the Wa, and the Kachin, who accepted the Bible as their lost book and became Christians as a result. The Hill tribes of Thailand and Myanmar are today the most Christianized groups in those two countries. The importance these people placed on the Lost Book legend is demonstrated by that fact.

Migration

Through interviews and articles, I have noticed one of the most consistent details recalled by Karen people regarding their origin is the areas they travelled through. Although dates and details vary, there seems to be some consensus that the Karen originated in the Middle East (Babylon is often cited) and then migrated to Tibet, Mongolia, the Gobi Desert (occasionally including Tajikistan), China, and finally south into Burma and Old Siam from Yunnan.

While genetics and archaeology offer no definitive answers, the persistence of connections between the Lost Book peoples suggests the dispersion of an ancient and literate people into Tibet, China, and then south to the Indian Ocean. Considering the similarities in cultural practices and oral traditions among the Karen and other tribes, the best candidate for the ancestors of such a people group is the exiled tribes of Israel.

Conclusion

The Karen people are a remarkable group whose identity as a people chosen of God has survived millennia. From the hills of Myanmar to refugee camps and global cities, they carry with them songs of Y'wa, memories of a lost golden book, and rituals that echo those of the ancient Israelites.

Bibliography

1. The Karen People of Burma: A Study in Anthropology and Ethnology by Rev Harry Ignatius Marshall. M.A. Copyright 1922, Ohio State University
2. Eternity in Their Hearts by Don Richardson Copyright 1981 by Regal Books
3. The Karen Apostle Or The Memoir of Koh Tha-Byu The First Karen Convert by Rev Francis Mason, Gould, Kendall, and Lincoln, 1843
4. The Karen of Burmah - A Remnant of the Ten Tribes of Israel, by Dr. Mason, Calcutta Christian Observer, May 1834
5. The Karen of Burmah - A Remnant of the Ten Tribes of Israel by Dr. Mason Part III, Calcutta Christian Observer, July 1835
6. Karen - Lost Tribes of Israel Golden Book and Other Traditions By Margot Crossing. Presented for Lost Tribes Institute 2nd Symposium, 9th & 10th May, 2024, Chiang Mai, Thailand
7. Between Hills and Plains. Power and Practice in Socio-Religious Dynamics among Karen by Hayami Yoko. Trans Pacific Press. February 1, 2004.
8. https://biblehub.com/topical/naves/c/captivity_of_the_ten_tribes.htm#:~:text=The%20Assyrian%20Empire%2C%20under%20the,of%20Pharaoh%20king%20of%20Egypt

Uzu Masa - A Banner for All Nations

By Richard Hewitt

Japan and Bible Forum & Lost Tribes Institute Symposium
Sept. 16, 2025, Tokyo, Japan

Acknowledgement

I am deeply grateful to Japan for this opportunity to speak to the dedicated scholars whose rigorous research inspires global understanding.

The Book

Dear Japan,

2500 years ago, the Great Ancestor of your "Tora no Maki" (Tora Scroll) said,

> For this is what the Lord Y'wa[1] says: I myself will search for my sheep and look after them. As a shepherd looks after his scattered flock when he is with them, so will I look after my sheep. I will rescue them from all the places where they were scattered on a day of clouds and darkness. I will bring them out from the nations and gather them from the countries, and I will bring them into their own land. (Ezekiel 34)

Did this "God Shepherd" bring us here to this symposium to discuss Israel's lost sheep? As I look around this symposium, many of the primary researchers follow Ishu, Uzu, Iso, Ise, Issa, Ieso, Iesu, Yaso, Yasho, Yaesu, Yeshua, Jesus, Jezi, or however you say the name in your culture and religion. It is reasonable to assume that this divine figure, known in every culture by culturally appropriate variations of his name, is the one who brought us together. We all read this Great Script, anthropology's most important text, because of our devotion to the Shepherd. While reading this text, we discovered Asia's cultural origins and critical diasporas.

---

[1] Ethnic Karen word for God. One of the symposium's speakers was ethnic Karen.

Kyrgyzstan

Now, let me introduce myself. While working with farmers in Kyrgyzstan in the 1990s, I noticed countless similarities between the Kyrgyz and this Book's customs.

- A chest like the ark of the covenant sits in the holiest part of every Kyrgyz home. This "sandyk" is about the same size as the Tabernacle's Ark described in Exodus.
- Like Moses' tabernacle and Solomon's temple, the Kyrgyz yurt is supposed to face east toward the rising sun. Likewise, those waiting for the Messiah expect him to return from the East (Matthew 24:27).
- Kyrgyz kill a lamb, just as Moses prescribed in Exodus 12; a perfect, one-year-old male, which they bleed, then cut at the joints, not cutting through the bones. They cut the lamb into 12 pieces, one for each tribe, even though they don't have 12 tribes. Supposedly, they once had 12 tribes.
- Kyrgyz also have odd sayings, like "There is no blessing on an empty plate," matching what Isaac demanded of his sons: "Prepare my favorite meal first, then I'll bless you." (Genesis 27)
- Kyrgyz have countless traditions like this.

I asked God why there were so many similarities. For a year, I was left without an answer. My list comparing Kyrgyz and ancient Israelites got longer, but since I had never recognized Israel's lost tribes in the Script, I looked elsewhere for a Kyrgyz-Israelite link. Some Kyrgyz scholars told me that Kyrgyz had lived in Syria and/or Egypt thousands of years ago, but there wasn't enough academic information to sway me.

Then I was in the mountains, drinking fermented horse milk alone in a yurt. The shepherd came in and started telling me the Kyrgyz oral epic "Manas." Manas is the Kyrgyz mythological hero.

- Manas, like Moses, led an exodus with 600,000 soldiers
- Like Joshua, he brought the people to their fatherland.
- Like Samson, he had great strength.
- Like David, he was a shepherd boy who killed a giant and became king.
- Manas's best friend, like David's friend Jonathan, was the son of the king who wanted to kill Manas.
- The Kyrgyz epic mirrors many more stories and typologies from Humanity's Great Script.

"Why God? Why so many similarities?"

The storyteller stopped his storytelling, leaned toward me, and asked, “Do you know the name of Manas’ father?”
“No,” I answered.
“Jakyb!” he said.

The Kyrgyz hero, Jakyb’s son Manas, is Jacob’s son Manasseh of the Great Book? The only place I hadn’t looked for evidence of a Kyrgyz-Israelite link was within the twelve tribes of Jacob, who is also known as Israel. (Benite, 2009)

In 2006, the Kyrgyz government invited me to their first international symposium to defend my comparison of their Jakyb and the Script’s Jacob.

- Both Jacobs are deceitful
- Both limp.
- Both complain about their unruly sons.
- Both nomadic Jakybs have two wives
- Both are faced with infertility.
- In both cases, God intervenes, and the barren wives give birth to a protagonist.
- Neither Jakyb is worthy of God’s blessing, but both are blessed.
- And the list of similarities continues. I wrote a book on this topic.

I quickly learned the Kyrgyz were from Israel’s Manasa Tribe. Understanding the Lost Tribes of Israel changed the way I read our planet’s Script and the way I looked at Kyrgyz history. Eventually, it changed the way I see all of human history and the planetwide network of cultures and religions. I also learned about some pseudo-religious Israelite movements: America’s Mormons, White supremacists, Black Hebrews, and even a Japanese movement from 100 years ago. These groups could have prevented their mistakes if they had simply kept this Holy Book’s Protagonist central to all they do. (Dever, 2024)

Additionally, Paul tells non-Jewish nations not to get circumcised. In other words, while telling them to trust Yeshua, he is telling nations not to enter Yeshua’s own religion! Why? Because if they did, they would be under all of the Jewish law and customs. That system is tough to navigate, even for those who grow up within the system. It would be unbearable for outsiders. Likewise, I don’t believe Japan’s youth should adopt the label “Christian,” which often carries Western cultural baggage, denominational complexities, foreign terminology, and a spirituality that doesn’t match Yeshua’s spirituality. Instead, this generation is invited to embrace Japan’s own messianic heritage with lives that reflect their Heavenly Sensei, Uzu Masa (Jesus), while also preparing for his return. By doing so, Japanese finally exalt the Yamato Damashii (Japanese spirit), returning to their Great Ancestor, Our Father in Heaven, and embracing their own Tora no Maki (虎の巻), the Script. Nothing else needs to be added.

Foundation

Japanese scholars diligently portrayed Japan's Israelite history. Others have exposed Siddhartha Gautama Buddha's potential connections to biblical traditions and Buddhism's spread among ancient Israelites (Chung, 2024), which broadened the scope of scripture's influence in Asia. Jesus' embodiment of Buddhist principles (Williams, 1988), the Jesus Sutras, and Pure Land Buddhism's parallels to New Testament teachings solidify the claims. This presentation focuses on Uzu Masa (太秦) as a unifying figure across Japan's history.

UzuMasa is a prominent location in Kyoto, which is Japan's ancient capital. A few Japanese scholars propose that the name UzuMasa, linked to the Hata clan, may reflect the Aramaic "Ishu Masha" (Yeshua ha Moshiach or Jesus the Messiah), suggesting a messianic connection in Japan's spiritual heritage. While historical and linguistic counterarguments exist, those defending the proposition have a strong case based on historical-linguistic studies (Saeki, 1908). Japan's ancient references to Yeshua don't stop with Uzu. Other Japanese names like Iso, Ise, Issa, Ieso, Yaso, Yasho, Yaesu, and other versions of Yeshua have been in Japan for hundreds of years. Yes, there is still debate on some of these names. Throughout Asia, waves of attacks have sought to erase much of Asia's rich messianic history (Jenkins, 2008). The remaining evidence in Japan indicates Uzu Masa's Japanese followers laid a solid foundation - a foundation to which modern Japanese must now respond.

Translation's Role

To present Uzu Masa as Japan's banner, I'll highlight the importance of translation. The Script, or Great Book, was originally written in three languages and was quickly translated into multiple regional languages. In the messianic era, translation is central. Humanity has thus developed dozens of localized and patriotic ways to name:

- God
- This Good Book,
- The Book's Protagonist - Yeshua, Ishu, Uzu, Jezi, Iesu, Yesu, Jesu, Gizu, Jesus
- And his titles, like Messiah, Moshiach, Mashayak, Masha, Mashi, Masa, Kristus, Logos, Lamb of God, and Amida. (Brown, 1999)

When words don't get translated (like Christ, Christian, Church, baptize, gospel, evangelize, or other foreign words), the whole text and its protagonist feel foreign and distant. Even the word "Christ" is a foreign word to a Westerner like me because I'm not Greek. Translating *Moshiach* as "The Anointed One" would have been a perfect translation in English. (Brown, 1999)

Jewish translators of the Greek Septuagint translated "Anointed One" from Hebrew "Messiah" to Greek "Christ." Great. But when translating the Script into Latin, they didn't translate "Christus" into Latin. Instead, they kept the "holy" Greek word. Eventually, every word in the Latin version became "too holy" to translate into common languages... so, the light of the Word was shrouded, and the Western world entered its Dark Ages. The West remained in darkness until it started translating the Book into local languages. (Tsumura, 2015)

Entitled One

Proper translation has caused the Anointed One to be titled with more titles than any other human. From the Script, we know that the title Messiah formed slowly through the centuries, like a seashell that grows undetected for years. The concept of Messiah starts in the early chapters of Genesis with a prophecy that the offspring of Eve would crush the serpent's head, and the serpent would strike the heel of Eve's offspring (Genesis 3). Scholars deduced that this defender would be born of a virgin, since the child wasn't listed as a seed of Adam. (Mitchell, 2016)

Through the centuries, images of Joseph, Moses, David, and Solomon were added to the growing picture of Messiah. Later prophecies about a Good Shepherd and others like it were added. Slowly, the shell (the concept) grew bigger and more beautiful. Finally, the shell was complete and left empty, for someone to fill. When Yeshua was born, he filled the space perfectly. The shell fit him as if made for him. Now, Messiah is Yeshua's title for eternity. (Morris, 1995)

When his message went to the Greek world, he took another ancient title, 'Logos', a philosophical and cosmological concept associated with Greek and Roman gods. Since winning the Logos (Word) title from its gods, he is also known globally as the Living Word.

He has continued gathering unique titles in countless cultures. The Mikir tribe calls him their Humble King (Sot Recho), who died and yet lives. To the Mizo and Karen, he is their legendary Coming King who restores peace and justice. The Sawi tribe of New Guinea titled him their reconciling Peace Child. In Altai, I call him Shunu, after their coming warrior-savior who will restore and translate their lost book. Central Asians have called him their sacred Wanderer (al-Khidr, Kydyr, or Hizr) for centuries. Southeast Asians created the concept of Amida Buddha (the Buddha of infinite light and life) for him. In Islam, he has been titled Mesikh, the Spirit of God (Ruhullah), and much more.

Tathagata in Buddhism, Sat Guru of Warrior Sikhs, Muktinath of Hindus, and the long-awaited Taheb of Samaritans. (Spinks, 2006) In Sanskrit, his name, Īśa (ईश), is placed as an epithet for major Hindu deities. Īśa or Īśvara is a title for Shiva and Vishnu. He completes the impossible feat of filling titles, typologies, epithets, and symbols from every religion and culture.

He is even called the Way, so I imagine we can call him the Beauty Way of Navajo, the Dao of Daoism, and the Shin-to (Spirit Way) of Shintoism. This ever-growing collection of international titles fits the Script's template, which honors him with more titles than just Messiah and Logos:
"Son of David"
"Lamb of God,"
"Prince of Peace,"
"Light of the World,"
"The Resurrection and Life"
"Bread of Life"
"The Way"
"Salvation of God,"
and much more.

Iso no kami shrine (石上神宮)

When I arrived at Kyoto's ancient Iso no kami shrine, I was fascinated that there was no idol at the place of worship. The spring for washing and a branch on the gate post with white origami paper reminded me of Central Asia's sacred sites. Since I had lived in Kyrgyzstan, I recognized "Iso" as an old name for Yeshua used by Poet Alisher Navoi (15th Century) and still used in Tajikistan. I asked my Japanese hosts what "Iso" meant.

From the *kanji* (logographic character), my hosts knew the ancient word stemmed from a sacred rock, but I was told that the *kanji* was difficult to decipher. I did more research and found that components of the "Iso" *kanji* also could imply the concept of "mouth" or "speaker". The is also a component (上) that could depict a rising man or deity, all aligning with the Tora no maki's (scripture's) portrayal of Iso (Uzu Masa). Other usages of 石上 initially complicated my understanding, but the components of Iso's *kanji* built an image of the Book's portrayal of Iso too compelling to ignore. Iso and the Book's messianic image that predated his birth are portrayed as a Rock or Cliff, a man, and "rising above," so each of the *kanji's* components is reflected in the scripture's depiction of Iso.

Shintoism's founders in Yamato (ancient name of Japan), may have been a Central Asian "*Yamat*" or "Jamat" (community) that migrated to Yamato and established their *Yamat* with Iso (Jesus) enshrined as Iso no Kami, "The God, Iso" or "Iso God" conveying images of a rising savior, sacred rock, and safe place.

So, with my Central Asian knowledge of Iso, I reverently went through the Iso no kami (Isonokami) gate, where white paper tied on a branch hanging on the gatepost reminded me of China's minority, the Qiang people, who place paper on a tree, indicating holiness. Tying paper on a tree branch also mirrors Kyrgyz tradition. Tearing cloth from their clothes, Kyrgyz tie it to a sacred tree at a sacred site as a means to transfer their sins from themselves to the tree. At the Iso no kami shrine, there was no idol, so I bowed, Japanese style, and prayed to Iso no Kami, the Rock who links Central Asia, China, and Japan, and vertically links Earth & Heaven. My Japanese actions in Japan felt right and pure. I didn't want to leave the Iso no kami shrine.

Kydyr

Among the Kyrgyz, Iso has also stepped into many symbols and titles like Messiah, Logos, Uzu Masa, and Iso no kami. My favorite Kyrgyz version is the mythical Wanderer (*Kydyr*).

Let me test you. I'll tell you Kyrgyz concepts of the *Kydyr*, and you tell me if that matches this book's depiction of Uzu Masa.

Kyrgyz say the *Kydyr* is their Road Partner on their journeys. Is there a match in the Good Book? Yes, Luke 24 says he joined two friends on the road to Emmaus. (Green, 1997)

- You might not recognize him when he comes to you. Is there a match?
- After he blesses you, he will disappear. There is a match in the Good Book.
- You must hold on to him until you get his blessing.
- He might ride a donkey into town.
- If you welcome *Kydyr* well, he will bless you. If you don't, you will lose your happiness.
- *Kydyr* is one of seven, meaning he might be in our midst now because there are more than seven of us here.
- The only way to identify *Kydyr* is by the hole, wound, or soft spot in his hand.

I have written that everything the Kyrgyz believe about their Kydyr can be matched to a verse within the Good Book. It's amazing. Japan's Ise, Iso, or Uzu is "Kydyr Isa" of the Kyrgyz, the one who is drawing Israel's scattered tribes to himself. He is not a foreigner in Asia.

> On that day, the Root of Jesse will stand as a banner for the peoples; the nations will rally to him, and his resting place will be glorious. On that day, the Lord will reach out his hand a second time to reclaim the surviving remnant of his people from Assyria, from Lower Egypt, from Upper Egypt, from Cush, from Elam, from Babylonia, from Hamath, and from the islands of the Mediterranean. He will raise a banner for the

> nations and gather the exiles of Israel; he will assemble the scattered people of Judah from the four quarters of the earth. (Isaiah 11:10-12)

Kanji

Every aspect of the Japanese culture and spirit aligns with the Protagonist of this Good Book, even the *kanji* 王 (ō), meaning king, mirrors a slightly more complex Kyrgyz "tamga" or tribal symbol. Both the Kyrgyz tamga and Japanese kanji "王" symbolize a mediator or leader/king linking the top "heavenly emperor" component with the lower "earth." The component between these two realms, connecting the two, is the controversial, international symbol of God's love for us, portrayed in the sacrifice of Japan's Sensei, Uzu Masa. (Henshall, 2014) This Japanese *kanji* embodies the text's ancient imagery, summed up in Philippians 2:6-9

> ... being found in appearance as a man, he (the king) humbled himself by becoming obedient to death—even death on a cross! Therefore God exalted him to the highest place and gave him the name that is above every name, that at the name of Uzu every knee should bow, in heaven and on earth and under the earth... (Philippians 2:6-9) (Lincoln, 1990)

Many other Japanese *kanji* and cultural treasures capture similar scriptural truths. Contrary to popular opinion, this Good Book and its Protagonist, Uzu, are not foreign to Japan. Take off the Western "Christian" packaging and you'll find the matured Yamato-damashii, Japan's spirit, within the pages of your Tora no maki, the ancient Torah Scroll. (Nitobe, 2002)

The Japanese Soul

Uzu Masa's Message on the Mount (Matthew 5-7) and foundational Japanese values resonate remarkably:

Happy are the poor in spirit...
Blessed are those who mourn - they will be comforted.
Blessed are the meek - they will inherit the earth.
Blessed are those who hunger and thirst for righteousness - they will be filled.
Blessed are the merciful - they will be shown mercy.
Blessed are the pure in heart - they will see God.
Blessed are the peacemakers - they will be called children of God.
Blessed are those who are persecuted for righteousness (Matthew 5:3-10) (Blomberg, 1992)

Uzu Masa's teachings in the scroll continue to resonate with Japan's culture and character, and align with both Shinto and Buddhist concepts of boundless compassion, inner purity, and the death of ego. (De Bary, 2005)

Similarly, Uzu Masa teaches us to "go the second mile", symbolizing *giri*, the Japanese moral obligation to exceed others' expectations, which I saw enacted by a Japanese follower of Uzu Masa days before this symposium. While Mr. Shimeki san showed us sites in Kyoto, a large rock shot from the mountain and hit him hard. He was down and couldn't get up. But then the *Yamato damashii* rose. I told him our team would be fine and his friends should take him to the hospital, but he wouldn't leave us until his task was completed. Despite immense pain, he and the other Japanese warriors went the second mile, and got us to UzuMasa and other fascinating sites in Kyoto, which they knew I had wanted to see. The Japanese went beyond what was expected. Countless similarities between Uzu and the Yamato Damashii exist.

I follow Hideo Hatakeda's social media. He argues that the moral code of Uzu Masa shares striking parallels with the ethical framework of the samurai, a perspective supported by scholarly analyses of *Bushidō*. These parallels suggest that much of the *Yamato-damashii* (大和魂), Japan's spirit, aligns with Uzu Masa's teachings, way, and life.

Pure Land Buddhism

At the heart of Pure Land Buddhism (Jōdo bukkyō), a Japanese branch of Mahayana Buddhism, lies a shared recognition of human limitation. Humanity needs a power beyond ourselves (*tariki*) to break the cycle and obtain enlightenment. In Jōdo bukkyō, the practitioners entrust themselves to Amida Buddha's mercy, acknowledging that liberation cannot be earned through effort but through the merit of Amida Buddha. The same is said of Uzu Masa - that salvation comes not from one's own goodness, but through trust in Uzu's goodness (*tariki*).

> "This is the work of God, to trust in the One He sent" (John 6:29)

Both buddhas (enlightened teachers), Amida and Uzu, promise salvation to the humble, the guilty, and the spiritually poor. They both offer liberation from the ego. (De Bary, 2005)

Amida as the Anointed One

Like the title Messiah, the concept of Amida Buddha also grew slowly over time. But unlike "Messiah," no historic figure fits Amida's title, "infinite light" and "infinite life." Does Uzu Masa fit that title? Can we call him Amida Iso or Amida Uzu? (Nagami, 2022)

The Good Book's smaller book of Colossians says all things were made for him and through him. Amida's narrative includes his pre-enlightenment form as Dharmakara, who vowed to create the Pure Land. Members of the Bible and Japan Forum (聖書と日本フォーラム), like Dr. Nagami, highlight that Dharmakara ("One who applies the Law/Truth"), Amida Buddha (Teacher of Infinite light and life), and the coming Maitreya, all share parallels with Uzu Masa, particularly in their roles as embodiments of divine truth. Like the Script's messianic prototype, Melchizedek, Dharmakara lacks a historical genealogy, suggesting a timeless, symbolic role that aligns with Melchizedek's messianic symbolism. (Nagami, 2022)

Amida means boundless. Pure Land Buddhism's Infinite Light (Amitābha) and Infinite Life (Amitāyus), preside over the Western Pure Land (Sukhavati). This title parallels Uzu Masa's life and titles, "Light of the World" (John 8:12) and "the Resurrection and Life" (John 11:25), destined to rule over Zion, which is to the West of Southeast Asia and Japan. (Nagami, 2022)

Just as the mythological Dharmakara eventually attained enlightenment, so Uzu also had to be transformed into perfection:

> Although he was a son, he learned obedience from what he suffered and, once made perfect, he became the source of eternal salvation for all who obey him" (Hebrews 5:8-9. Also note Hebrews 2:10).

Uzu Masa is Amida and the fulfillment of Pure Land Buddhism. One can read about his sufferings and teachings in the Good Book. This perspective invites Japanese readers to see Uzu Masa not as a foreign figure but as central to their spiritual heritage, fostering a return to national identity and a renewal of Japan's meaningful traditions. The Ancient Text does not support conversion to Christianity, Judaism, or another foreign religion, but a return to true Shintoism, the ancient God Path of Japan's ancestors.

While suffering immensely and facing certain death, Uzu told his followers to love their enemies and then forgave those who were killing him. His historic biography embodies the core tenets of Amida and provides a real flesh-and-blood example for Pure Land Buddhists.

Remarkably, Uzu Masa has done what is expected of him in every aspect of Japanese culture. He has earned the titles Amida Buddha and Dharmakara. He is the way of Shintoism and encompasses the goal of Pure Land Buddhism. These beautiful Japanese "shells" were prepared for him. (Nagami, 2022)

Torii

Uzu Masa declares, "I am the Torii (gate); whoever enters through me will find salvation" (John 10:9). Japan's elegant Torii, marking the sacred threshold in Shinto tradition, mirrors Uzu's role as the gateway to divine peace, inviting all to pass through into God's boundless Pure Land.

In Israel's history, during the Passover, God instructed the Israelites to mark their wooden doorposts and lintel with the blood of an innocent lamb. Death would "pass over" every household that bore this blood, whether the occupants were worthy or not. These blood-stained doorways, emblematic of Torii, became the earliest symbols of salvation through substitution - *tariki*.

Ultimately, Amida Buddha needs a human embodiment because the unworthy are not worthy of the pure land. Japan's youth know that. We have all been liars, cheats, thieves, and haters. The Great Ancestor is perfectly just and must respond to our evil in a visible manner. Injustice can't be wiped away without a just response, the spilling of blood; otherwise, there is no cosmic balance, no pure land, and no end to the cycle (*samsara*). Uzu's flesh and blood sacrifice on our behalf balances the universe and settles our doubts. Blood has spilled on our behalf. Payment for injustice is paid in full. The *samsara* is stopped. The unworthy, now cleansed and forgiven, won't stain the Pure Land. Pure Land Buddhism is summed up in the following phrase:

> "For God so loved the world, that he gave his only Son, that whoever believes in him should not perish but have eternal life." (John 3:16)

An elegant Torii, marking the sacred threshold in Shinto tradition, mirrors Uzu's role as the gateway to divine peace, inviting all to pass through into God's boundless Pure Land. Uzu is the sole passage into God's boundless Pure Land. Those who pass through Uzu, Heaven's Torii, find enlightenment, not through deeds or rituals but through faith in the hero's righteousness and self-sacrifice. Yes, the old guardians might be upset by this application, but Japan's first loyalty is not to them, but to Uzu Masa. Today is the day to return to Japan's original faith by passing through the Torii. Today is the day to raise Japan's banner.

Conclusion

In conclusion, Uzu Masa is central to many cultures and religions, with countless titles enshrining him as the Good Shepherd and Japan's Torii. He unites ancient prophecy, Japanese spirituality, global cultural narratives, historic migrations, and interfaith religious practices. By embracing the Great Script in its culturally resonant form, Japan can rediscover its spiritual heritage, fulfilling the vision of Isaiah 11 where all nations rally to the Messiah as God's banner.

Bibliography

Benite, Z. B.-D. (2009). The ten lost tribes: A world history. Oxford University Press.

Blenkinsopp, J. (1996). A history of prophecy in Israel. Westminster John Knox Press.

Blomberg, C. L. (1992). Matthew. The New American Commentary, Vol. 22. Broadman Press.

Bowring, Richard. *The Religious Traditions of Japan: 500-1600*. Cambridge University Press, 2005.

Brown, C. (Ed.). (1999). New international dictionary of New Testament theology. Zondervan.

Chung, H.-S. (2024). Links between Korea, Southeast China, and Southeast Asia. In R. Hewitt, M. Skobac, & Y. Rambsel (Eds.), Lost Tribes Institute's 2nd international symposium (pp. 37–50). Amazon Digital Services LLC - KDP.

De Bary, W. T. (Ed.). (2005). Sources of Japanese tradition: Volume 2, 1600 to 2000. Columbia University Press.

Dever, W. G. (2024). The ten lost tribes of Israel aren't lost (and never were). Biblical Archaeology Review, Winter 2024.

Eidelberg, J. (2014). The Japanese and the ten lost tribes of Israel. Gefen Publishing.

Green, J. B. (1997). The Gospel of Luke. The New International Commentary on the New Testament. Eerdmans.

Halpern, J. (2008). New Japanese-English character dictionary. Kenkyusha.

Hatakeda, H. (2023-2025). Personal communication.

Henshall, K. G. (2014). A guide to learning kanji. Tuttle Publishing.

Jenkins, Philip. *The Lost History of Christianity: The Thousand-Year Golden Age of the Church in the Middle East, Africa, and Asia—and How It Died.* HarperOne, 2008.

Kubo, A. (2004). Israelites came to ancient Japan. Remnant Publishing. http://www2.biglobe.ne.jp/~remnant/israel.htm

Kubo, Arimasa. "Japanese-Israeli Common Ancestry Theory." *YouTube Lectures and Articles*, various dates.

Kume, Kunitake. *Nihon Shoki and Historical Records*. 1880s, republished in various formats.

Lincoln, A. T. (1990). Ephesians. Word Biblical Commentary, Vol. 42. Word Books.
Mitchell, D. C. (2016). *Messiah ben Joseph*. Campbell Publications.
Moo, D. J. (1996). The epistle to the Romans. The New International Commentary on the New Testament. Eerdmans.
Morris, L. (1995). The Gospel according to John. The New International Commentary on the New Testament. Eerdmans.
Nagami, K. (2022). Japanese and Jews: Exploring Hebrew traditions in Shintoism. In R. Hewitt, M. Crossing, et al. (Eds.), The interconnectedness of Israel in Asia: Book two (pp. 45–60). Amazon Digital Services LLC - KDP.
Nitobe, I. (2002). Bushido: The soul of Japan. Kodansha International. (Original work published 1900)
Oswalt, J. N. (1998). The Book of Isaiah, Chapters 40–66. The New International Commentary on the Old Testament. Eerdmans.
Saeki, Y. (1908). Kirishitan bunko. Waseda University Press.
Saeki, Yoshiro. *Keikyō hibun kenkyū* [Studies on Nestorian Inscriptions]. 1911.
Seward, J. (1992). Japanese in action: An unorthodox approach to the spoken language and the people who speak it. Weatherhill.
Shogakukan. (2003). Shogakukan progressive Japanese-English dictionary. Shogakukan.
Spinks, G. S. (2006). Theological Dictionary of the New Testament: Abridged in one volume. Eerdmans Publishing.
Teshima, Ikuro. *The Ancient Jewish Diaspora in Japan: The Tribe of Hata*. Japan, 1973.
Tsumura, D. T. (2015). Theological terms in Japanese: A study of biblical translation. Journal of Japanese Studies, 41(2), 305–328.
Williams, J. G. (1988). Yeshua Buddha: An interpretation of New Testament theology as a meaningful myth. Quest Books.
The Holy Bible, New International Version (NIV). (2011). Zondervan.

Made in the USA
Las Vegas, NV
18 October 2025

32510648R00050